love /

X - mass ~~75~~

Visions of
SNOWDONIA

Visions of
SNOWDONIA

Landscape and Legend

Jim Perrin

Photographs by Ray Wood

Foreword by
Anthony Hopkins

BBC BOOKS

For William Condry and Dr Enid Pierce Roberts,
best of teachers

FRONTISPIECE The great dolmen of Maen y Bardd
(the poet's stone) has stood for 5000 years alongside the ancient
line of communication between Dyffryn Conwy and the west.
A neolithic burial site, the landscape around it abounds in
prehistoric features. The trackway which passes by was
'improved' as long ago as Roman times.

This book accompanies the series *Visions of Snowdonia*
produced by BBC Wales and first broadcast in 1997.
Executive producer: Phil George · Director: Graham Johnston
Researcher: Meic Birtwistle

Designed by BBC Books and Andrew Shoolbred
Maps © Line & Line (Geographical data © RH Publications 1996)

ISBN 0 563 38302 X

First published in Great Britain in 1997
Published by BBC Books, an imprint of BBC Worldwide Publishing
BBC Worldwide Limited, Woodlands, 80 Wood Lane
London W12 OTT

Jacket printed by Lawrence Allen Limited, Weston-super-Mare
Colour separations by Radstock Reproductions,
Midsomer Norton
Printed and bound by Butler & Tanner Limited,
Frome and London

CONTENTS

Anglesey

A5

A4080

A5

Penmaenmawr
Llanfairfechan
② Bangor

A55

Conwy

A5

Afon Conwy

Conwy

A470

A548

Bethesda
*Carnedd
Llewelyn* △
Cwm y Glo
△ *Carnedd Dafydd*

A548

Caernarfon **③**

A5

Llanberis
Tryfan △
*Llyn
Ogwen*
Llanrwst

A4085

Glyder Fawr △△
Capel Curig
A543

A4086
△ *Glyder
Fach*
*Moel
Siabod* △
Betws y Coed

Nantlle
Snowdon
Dolwyddelan

Gwynedd
A498
A470
Pentrefoelas
A5

Beddgelert **④**
*Llyn
Conwy*
Ysbyty Ifan

*Lleyn
Peninsula*
A499
Blaenau
Ffestiniog **①**
Migneint

A487
Arenig Fach △

A497
*Llyn
Trawsfynydd*
A4212
*Llyn
Celyn*

Porthmadog
A470
Trawsfynydd
Bala
Llyn Tegid

Harlech
Afon Mawddach
Llanuwchllyn
A494

*Rhinog
Fawr* △
Llangynog

A496
Llyn Efyrnwy

⑤
A470

Barmouth
Dolgellau
A458

△ *Cadair Idris*
Mallwyd
A487
A458

Tal y Llyn
Corris

Afon Dyfi

Tywyn
A493
A487
A470

Machynlleth

*Boundary of Snowdonia
National Park*
① *Start of journey*
Route
Roads
Railways

0   10 M

0   10 Km

FOREWORD

I love Snowdonia. It is not my home country, my patch, because I was raised in industrial South Wales. But it has come to haunt me, as it has many travellers and walkers before me. It is a powerful uncompromising land, a fortress whose ramparts guard an old language and an old people. But it is also a place of invitation, with hidden valleys and glassy lakes stretching forever into the blue. And in slate quarries or climbing tracks, in castles or in sheepfolds, it bears the marks of human survival and desire.

Jim Perrin has written a book full of affection and respect for Snowdonia. It is a portrait crafted by knowledge and love. He has climbed the high peaks and strolled along quiet pathways not used by more casual visitors. He cares for the people, for their culture and language, as much as for rocks and stones and trees. There is an intimacy and freshness in this writing which avoids the inflations that often come when trying to describe great landscapes. And he knows the fun and roguishness of the place too.

I have for several years had the honour to be President of the National Trust Snowdonia Appeal. As the largest landowner in the Snowdonia National Park, the Trust has to show care for small tenant farmers and their survival, as much as for conservation of natural beauty and the needs of tourists who swarm to the honeypot sites. It is a balancing act, to meet the huge hunger for wilderness and yet to preserve land and culture. *Visions of Snowdonia,* both book and television series, bear witness to the crucial importance of this venture for all of us.

INTRODUCTION

My home is in the Welsh mountains, and has been since I was free to make that choice. I'm tied here not just by blood – my grandparents were Denbighshire Welsh who, like generations before them, left their home-place with the economic migrants seeking work in England, South Wales or elsewhere in the early years of this century – but by unshakable bonds of affection and, more than that, entrancement. This mountainous region at the western margin of the British mainland is to me the most beautiful and various of countries, and the most miraculous too in terms of its history, cultural resistance and continuing survival as a place with an identity apart from its conquering, subsuming, more affluent eastern neighbour.

To be Welsh, to assume the mantle of this national identity, historically has been to invite ridicule and mistrust. You need look no further than Shakespeare or consider the verb 'to welsh' to see that response in operation. It has long seemed to me that the underlying explanation of this is reaction against foreignness. For whatever else Wales is, it is not England, it is *other*. Even its English name (remember that to its own people Wales is Cymru, 'our land') derives from the Saxon word *weallas*, meaning foreigners. Wales is different, older in its culture, its parallel history reflecting on without morally illuminating that of England.

This mockery proceeding from underlying unease persists, for the most part as a vague sense only. But it is highlighted by a few crucial factors, of which perhaps the most significant is the retention of a different language as a living entity in the region the Welsh call *Y Fro Gymraeg*, the Welsh Home-land (Snowdonia, or Eryri to give it the Welsh name, comprises an important part of this). Because the language is not immediately accessible, because its strange groupings of apparent consonants are incomprehensible to the unacquainted and the unaware, the proudly monoglot Saxons (the Welsh word for Englishmen is still *Saeson*) stand on their dignity and all too often bluffly reject it. If they move into the area, they frequently complain, ignoring all statistics, of the effect of this linguistic antique on their children's schooling, when they might more justifiably consider the ill effects of their presence on a culture older, more vital, and more integrated into the lives of its communities than their own.

I don't know whether the Welsh language can survive as anything other than an atavistic oddity in a transactional, post-industrial society. But I hope it does, for language carries more weight than that required for the skills of contemporary communication. There are, as I mentioned, other factors at work here too. It would be ostrich-like to deny the lingering subliminal resentment in Wales of its status as a long-conquered nation. Stir in depopulation, Calvinism, economic deprivation and environmental despoliation, and reasons for friction and distance become all too readily apparent. It is such a pity. The Welsh language and its literature forms one of the great cultural gifts of Europe, in its character and particularly in its poetry of a unique and singular beauty. Even the sound and meaning of place-names, if the effort is made to discover and translate, are a form of topographically descriptive poetry transcending anything east of the border. I not only hope that Welsh will not die, I do not believe that it will. It comprehends too much of value for that ever to be allowed to happen.

This book is a celebration of that value, and of Snowdonia's richness, history, cultural texture and beauty. It's an attempt to promote a better understanding of our country to visitors, and to remind those who live here of – and give them confidence in – its astonishing, lovely diversity. It also seeks to give some sense of the immediate landscape. When I'm away from Wales, I find myself often longing for so simple a thing as the sage-green or the orange or the may-green lichens of a Welsh mountain or seaward slope, adorning rock the colour of quicksilver or hard and veiny as seasoned timber and clean as the wind. When I think of Wales, I do not think of its obvious distinctions – its palpable sense of history and loss, the difficult harmonics of

OVERLEAF The peak of Tryfan (*tri faen* – three stones) – the rockiest south of the Scottish border – rises abruptly to a summit which is 600 metres above, and only half-a-mile from, the A5 road. It has the reputation of being the only mountain on mainland Britain which cannot be ascended without the use of hands.

its language, its otherness – but more of its smaller detail. There are the streams to which, if you were led blindfold, ignorant and disorientated, you could never mistake for a Lakeland beck. 'Look,' say the rocks through which the streams bridle and thrill their way, 'we are *Welsh* rocks. Geology itself has borrowed the names of our tribes: Silurian, Ordovician, Pre-Cambrian. And look at the ferns, look at the flowers which adorn us. Where else would you find these riches?'

There are the arctic-alpine flowers too. Each spring I go into the mountains to find them, to see what is growing, and where, and in what quantity. I go to Clogwyn Du'r Arddu high on Snowdon, perhaps, with the mist louring so that the mountain's dark, sheer faces loom above and the swirl of vapour, by tricks of perspective, transfers movement and gargoyle trickery to the rocks. Out of the greyness and obscurity, suddenly you see a glimmer of colour; you approach it, and there are the fleshy leaves and yellow flowers of rose-root hanging down, or the pinks and purples of saxifrages and moss campion, or the delicate white grace of the Snowdon lily, or thyme spreading, simply. And to see them there, so small and fine in such a savage place, fills you with a beneficent sense of marvels.

It's odd the extent to which we neglect our aesthetic sense of the land, and yet surely, as in art, it is a subject worthy of discussion and susceptible to definition: John Ruskin tried it 150 years ago; he was laughed to scorn by the prosaic and scientifically self-justifying members of the mountaineering community of his day when he dared to suggest that mountains were perhaps finer to look at than to look from. But there are times when I have a distinct sense that there is a validity in his argument. I think of the hills of North Wales in terms of their outline and their tonal range, for example. My memory and imagination fix momentarily on the sharp, pyramidal symmetries of Cnicht, with the falls and flow of the Afon Croesor washing the foreground and the oakwoods of the valley sides intensifying the texture of the scene. Or I think of any one of a dozen different perspectives on Tryfan, or the way in which the line of the crest of the hills that enclose Cwm Pennant to the north-west, a line visible from so many locations in central and western Snowdonia, imprints itself upon my awareness and sense of the place so that the recollection – just of that outline, nothing more – cuts in with the loveliest clarity time and again in the mundane and dreary moments of living. These things bring relief and release. It is important to let them register, to acknowledge them, and for me it is from the landscape of Wales that all the crucial images – 'Felt in the blood, and felt along the heart,/And passing even into my purer mind/With tranquil restoration' – derive.

As I ponder thus, what comes through to me most clearly is the ache and depth of love this country inspires in me, the way in which threats and affronts to it, dismissals of its quality, are assimilated into my consciousness as an almost physical hurt. I have a passion for this place, call it the country of my heart, look at it always in that surprised, wondering, curious and compassionate way in which, equally, your gaze might fix in rare moments on a person whom you love. Except that, unlike those other affairs, this relationship has lasted most of my life, it is in no sense jealous or exclusive – and here it is for you to share, who will know also that love implies recognition, caring and respect.

CHAPTER ONE

BORDER

At one point on the road between Ysbyty Ifan and Llan Ffestiniog, if you're travelling east, you're attentive, and the mist which often extinguishes this landscape's sense of space is not down, you should catch a momentary glimmer of water among the brown or purple ridges to the north-east. Since all journeys must have a beginning, it's here that we'll start ours around the heartland of North Wales.

The water is called Llyn Conwy. On the map, it tugs at your attention from among tracts of apparently featureless moorland. In shape and orientation, it's rather like a map of Africa with the extremities – the jut of the Horn, the bulging Sahara, the droop of the Cape of Good Hope – accentuated. There, the similarity ends, for this landscape is unique. It is not pretty; it has none of the vivacity or surface attraction of places we will come to, even quite soon. But it has its appeal. Travellers in former centuries would no doubt have thought it desolate, and so, in strict human definition, it is. Except that desolate also means devoid of comfort, and this wild, wide and empty space is not that. For those qualities, that sense of *tabula rasa* which hovers about it, are a profound spiritual comfort in our necessary retreats from the urbanized world.

There are two obvious routes to Llyn Conwy. One is a fisherman's path from the west which zig-zags through the quagmires from the isolated

Springtime in the valley of the Afon Rhaeadr Fawr

cottage of Hafodyredwydd to drop down to the northern shore. The second is a smooth, grassy track rising gradually through heather interspersed with patches of gleaming emerald sphagnum moss from the lonely former game-keeper's house by Pont ar Gonwy. Both of them start from narrow roads traversing this great emptiness, and head off into terrain which promises nothing, where the windy silences are disturbed only by the whirring grouse with their harsh calls. Even the skylark and the curlew seem to have abandoned this place. Yet suddenly you arrive at a scene of great power, where landscape itself seems gathered into the process of beginning.

The lake is high – a sheet of water maybe a kilometre across on either axis, at an altitude of nearly 500 metres. Many of the high peaks of Snowdonia appear above the encircling rim of moor, and from here, because of the scale of the surroundings and the lack of depth brought by the concealment of their valleys, they appear relatively insignificant. It is the lake itself which captivates. This is landscape reduced to primal, tonal qualities, water which takes on sky-hue and inflects it with its own atmosphere. On cloudy days it lies in pewter sullenness. Wind and a blue sky fleck it with bold, white strokes of waves. Even the names on the map share this reduced quality: Bryniau Duon, Bryn Crwn, Waen Fraith, Llechwedd Bryniau Defaid (Black Hills, Round Hill, Speckled Moor, Slatey-faced Hills of Sheep).

It's surprisingly unmeddled-with by the extractors of water. The lake level is the same as when first surveyed at the beginning of the last century, the bleached rocks and promontories of its shoreline as they have always been. Ready availability of motor transport, or perhaps the enforcement of regulations by the water authority that uses it as a reservoir, has rendered redundant fishermen's and bailiffs' huts, the former of which a guidebook writer forty years ago described as 'simply furnished with tables and chairs and a rudimentary kitchen and other amenities for the fishing sojourner'.

You might imagine it quiet but it is not. Gulls and terns which nest on small, rocky islets make it cacophonous and the air is seldom still, the wind breathy among sedge and red moor-grasses even on calm days. We start our

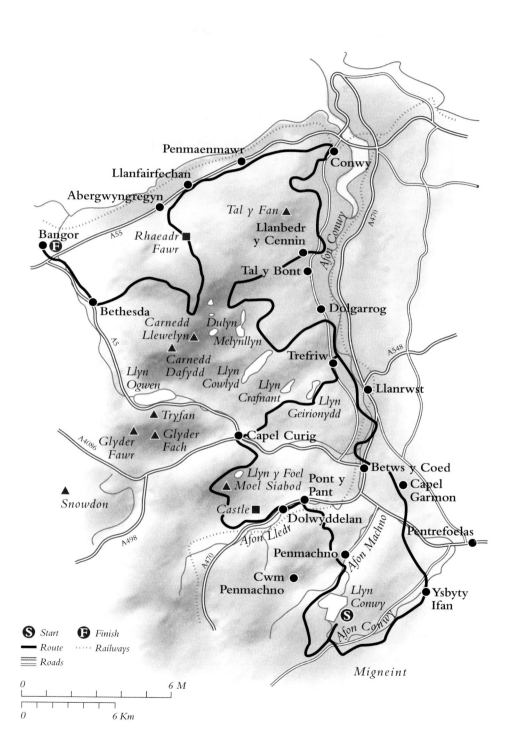

Tal y Fan ▲

Penmaenmawr
Conwy
Llanfairfechan
Abergwyngregyn
Llanbedr y Cennin
Bangor 🅵
Rhaeadr Fawr
Tal y Bont
Bethesda
Dolgarrog
Carnedd Llewelyn ▲
Dulyn
Melynllyn
Carnedd Dafydd
Trefriw
Llyn Ogwen
Llyn Cowlyd
Llyn Crafnant
Llanrwst
Tryfan ▲
Llyn Geirionydd
Glyder Fawr ▲ Glyder Fach ▲
Capel Curig
Snowdon ▲
Betws y Coed
Llyn y Foel Moel Siabod ▲
Pont y Pant
Capel Garmon
Castle ■
Dolwyddelan
Pentrefoelas
Afon Lledr
Penmachno
Afon Machno
Cwm Penmachno
Llyn Conwy
Ysbyty Ifan
Afon Conwy
🆂
Migneint

🆂 Start   🅵 Finish
━━ Route   ⋯ Railways
≡ Roads

0 ————— 6 M
0 ————— 6 Km

journey here not only because it is the table of landscape standing empty, ready to receive our visions, stories and interpretations, but also because this elevated lake, immunized by situation against the rash of tourism, as its waters break southwards between the mottled thighs of the moor gives birth to the river which describes for us a boundary and a route to be followed.

The Afon Conwy – River Conway in English – gives no hint in its infancy of its historical importance as barrier to successive invasions. It starts life as a peat-brown, rushing stream which, within a twisting mile, has received its first significant tributary, the Afon Ddu, the various branches of which drain the sodden peat of the Migneint. Like many Welsh rivers, the Conwy's sense of direction is questing and perverse. At first it wanders southwards before tippling itself over tilted strata into a valley that curves to the north-east. In a little over twenty miles as the crow flies – twice that as the river flows – it will meander due north to the sea.

In the journey to reach the river's mouth, you can follow the first road that crosses it – at Pont ar Gonwy – in two directions. To the west, you leave the river behind and cross country of astonishing solitude. The poet and experimental novelist B.S. Johnson set a bizarre and disturbing ghost story – a variation on the phantom hitch-hiker theme involving a *sheelagh-na-gig* – on this stretch of road, and if you drive this way on a rainswept winter's night, knowledge of it could cause you a few qualms. In sunlight, the tutelary presences are more benign, the peaks of Arenig Fawr, Arenig Fach and Moel Llyfnant presenting themselves to great advantage above quartzy, abrupt out-crops and broad horizons. Within a couple of miles an even narrower road branches north by a small, roofed enclosure, which contains a stone basin of cold spring water. In an interesting reversion to superstition, coins are to be

A solitary fisherman drifts across the still waters of Llyn Conwy at dawn. This high, remote lake, in surroundings of astonishing bleakness, is one of the least visited places in Snowdonia, invariably deserted and silent except for the incessant squabbling of gulls which nest on its heathery islets.

found in it with increasing frequency these days – and so too, in the tourist season, are small boys fishing for them, having bicycled the five miles up from Ffestiniog or Penmachno. An inscription on a tablet above reads: *'Ffynnon Eidda 1846 – Yf a bydd Ddiolchgar'*. Ffynnon Eidda is the name of the well, the rest means 'drink and be thankful'.

One thing to be profoundly thankful for is not to have been a leper in the Middle Ages, for at the opposite corner of this bleak quadrant of moor formerly stood the *tŷ lasar*, the lepers' quarantine house endowed by the hospice of the Knights of St John of Jerusalem at Ysbyty Ifan. After the suppression of the order Y Dylasar passed into the hands of the Lloyd family, one of whom was the Bishop of Bangor Humphrey Lloyd (1610-1689), a covetous and unpleasant character who makes a comic-sinister appearance in the pages of Anthony Wood's testy biographical dictionary of 1692 *Athenae Oxonienses*. Lloyd mounted a notable, though self-interested, rearguard action against evangelism in Wales and particularly the activities of Thomas Gouge (1605-1681), whose Welsh Trust aimed to provide education in English for Welsh children and a new translation of the Bible into Welsh. In opposing these, Lloyd unwittingly contributed to the perpetuation of the Welsh language and the eventual native vigour of the dissenting movement in Wales, as well as preserving in common usage the great masterpiece of Welsh prose style which is the translation of the Bible by William Morgan – the second bishop to hail from this small geographical area, and one whose birthplace we shall shortly visit.

The road north from Ffynnon Eidda slants down across a hillside extensively marred by dark, regular plantations of spruce and Douglas fir into the valley of the Afon Machno at the terraced hamlet of Carrog, whence it runs alongside meadows where properly green native grass, as opposed to the blue-rinsed Euro-varieties, is spangled with buttercup and cowslip, meadowsweet and eyebright. The village of Cwm Penmachno, at the valley head, is a claustrophobic assembly of tight terraces under the sprawl of old slate workings. These formerly connected through with quarries at Manod, on the other side of the hill, and the underground workings were beloved of television directors and groups from outdoor centres until a serious accident befell one of the latter and their use was banned. In the war some of these subterranean galleries were used for the storage of art treasures, and local rumour holds that others are put to continuing and more mysterious security purposes. Whatever the truth may be, the place, with its gloomy conifers, derelict industry and plethora of 'For Sale' signs, doesn't offer much incitement to linger.

Penmachno is the main village of this long side valley off that of the Conwy. It's a cluster of attractive, tiny, terraced houses, ornate chapelry and a large churchyard, all threaded through by narrow lanes and the wide, shallow stream, crossed here by an agreeably primitive five-arched bridge, whose dedicatory stone, dating from 1785, shows two pipe-smoking men who may or not be its builders, Ieuan Hughes and Harry Parry of Caernarfon. It's rather endearing to imagine the architects knocking out the bowls of their clay pipes on the parapet while contemplating the completion of their work on some fine summer evening with the water trickling past over the pebbles, the sun dipping below the rim of Glasgwm and the moorhens calling.

In the Dark Ages, Penmachno, in its hidden valley, appears to have been an ecclesiastical centre of some importance. The nineteenth-century church, within its oval churchyard, is the third on the site. In the walls of its twelfth-century predecessor, and elsewhere in the valley, were found inscribed stones from the fifth or early sixth centuries, which have given scholars numerous clues both to the status of the establishment here and to Latin usage of the period. The font in the Victorian church is a crudely fashioned block of granite from the twelfth century, and both the church and the village's holy well (which is oddly situated in the cellar of the old post office), are dedicated to St Tudclud, who is unfortunately not one of those Celtic saints about whom a rich tradition of story survives.

If you opt to cross the afforested ridge from Penmachno into the valley of the Afon Lledr – the largest of the Conwy's tributaries – this ecclesiastical

CLYDE HOLMES

If it hadn't been for George's sore shoulder, Clyde Holmes, his wife and family, might never have come to Cwm Hesgyn. George was a shire horse, pulling Clyde and Gudrun in a caravan around Ireland. There were scheduled stops each night at which a farmer would take off George's harness and, the next morning, put it back on and adjust it. But Clyde departed from the itinerary, went his own way. At Leenaun down in Connemara unskilled hands had set leather too tight against the horse's shoulder, caused it to rub raw, and they had been brought to a halt. Which is where they learnt, fortuitously, about an estate near Bala with isolated houses to let. The first two they were shown were unsuitable. When, as an afterthought, the estate came up with a cottage on the verge of dereliction a mile or more up a track off the main road, Clyde and Gudrun both knew.

For Clyde, 'it was definitely right – you just know'. For Gudrun, the drive up had reminded her of parts of Germany she knew as a child. They took it on in 1970. The last resident, a shepherd, had left in March 1947. When the great snow of that winter engulfed the house, he'd escaped through a skylight, walked on the tops of walls to the road and had never come back. Clyde and Gudrun worked on the house to make it habitable. In 1973 they moved in with their year-old daughter Malka. They've been there ever since, adding a son, Beorn, to the family along the way – he now studies each day in Wrexham. Malka, whom Gudrun educated at home, has taken a fine art degree in Leeds and is hoping to go on to the Slade. And Clyde, having found his inspiration here, works on.

He's fifty-six now, a spare, intense, detached man whose black hair is flecked with grey at the temples. In the 1960s he studied at Hornsey College and St Martin's School of Art and afterwards, because he didn't want to 'go into art', worked at the Royal National Institute for the Blind. Perhaps that experience of seeing the world interpreted and experienced through touch led him to desire for his own art this closer touch with the earth. His whole artistic project – the large canvases, the jewelled poems – seems in process of focusing ever more closely; you start from skyscapes of towering, dramatic clouds hachured in grey and flashed with blue and, moving the attention, con-centrating the discipline of looking, you are led down to slopes of heather and rushes lit and shaded into a swirl of abstraction. When you ask about influence, he talks of the writers W. H. Hudson and Richard Jefferies. Like the landscape in which he works, the paintings are stripped of humanity. He has moved into the skin of the planet to record texture and detail. Best to let him explain in his own words:

An ever-increasing tourist trade is 'buying and selling' Wales, wetlands are detroyed, riverbeds altered, roads widened and whole fields converted into campsites: the leisure industry is taking its toll. Many ecologists believe that flora, fauna and even indigenous people will only be able to survive in small, protected 'islands', be it rainforest, tundra or moorland as the ever-increasing greed of humanity will use and destroy most wild areas by the turn of the century. Cwm Hesgyn and its immediate surroundings is one of these 'islands'. I feel that my concern and love for it is best conveyed through painting and poetry. I use as few words as possible as I like to express the restraint and simplicity of a day at Cwm Hesgyn where light, or the lack of it, is a vital feature. I have tried to do the same in my paintings, exploring the uplands and its solitude. I'm committed to expressing the wildness of Welsh landscape for its own sake, its left-aloneness. It is essentially an unfixed mysterious place with light and shadow constantly moving over its surface. I am always shifting my preoccupations to paint this ephemeral flux...

theme is continued as you come across Tŷ Mawr Gwybrnant, a lovely seven-teenth-century stone house that has tiny irregular mullioned windows and high, listing chimneystacks. It faces the morning sun in a cottage garden with Welsh poppies, meadow cranesbill and hollyhocks, lying among meadows where orchids proliferate in June, and looking out to Mynydd Hiraethog, beneath which, at Llanelwy (St Asaph), lies the last bishopric and resting place of Gwybrnant's most famous son. For Tŷ Mawr was built on the birth-place of William Morgan (1545-1604), whose single-handed translation of the Bible into Welsh, as scholars of that language will delight in telling you, was published in 1588, thus pre-dating the King James Bible by twenty-three years. Morgan undertook the task as a poor and beleaguered parish priest in the Montgomeryshire village of Llanrhaeadr ym Mochnant. Without benefit of library or collaborative support he produced a literary masterpiece, sure-eared, accurate and majestic, which fixed and perpetuated the language in which it was written. Mention of Morgan is apt to inspire reverence amongst the Welsh, and that this eventual bishop in an age of canonical greed died a poor man suggests that the response is appropriate. Tŷ Mawr is now owned and has been sympathetically restored by the National Trust, which has created an exhibition here on William Morgan's life.

A sequence of gates slows progress from Gwybrnant down into the Lledr Valley, and it's well worth quitting the road to take the footpath which leads beyond Tanaeldroch into the gorge of the river. There is a precarious and exciting fishermen's walk through this to Pont y Pant – rickety horizontal ladders are supported on steel rods drilled into sheer rock walls above deep, swirling pools. Dappled light from the water reflects up on to mosses and ferns, the deadly hemlock water dropwort sprouts from moist crannies and clumps of purple-flowered chives – presumably garden escapes – flourish on midstream boulders. Mauves and ochres of riverbed stones, the dipping, long-tailed flight of a yellow wagtail after the biplane cruise of a sage-green dragon-fly, and the hypnotic circling of grass trapped in an eddy until the waters rise, all add to the allure of this most secret and exquisite place.

Medieval chronicles record that a squirrel, if it were so minded, could travel from branch to branch of the oak trees all the way from Conwy to Dolwyddelan without once touching the ground, so thick was the forest. Riparian growth apart, there's little of it left now in the valley of the Afon Lledr. Climatic change and the coming of the all-devouring sheep took their toll, and the supplanting spruce has been too heavily planted. There are no red squirrels either, though the last time I saw one in the National Park was just above Dolwyddelan twenty years ago; it ran along a wall and was close enough almost to touch. But this valley is still one of the most spectacularly lovely in Snowdonia. I remember driving back from a holiday in the Dordogne by way of Brittany, Wiltshire, the Wye Valley and the Welsh Marches to arrive here, where I then lived, on a golden autumn afternoon. The glowing brocade of relict woodland, with Moel Siabod's peak a shapely silver above, made up the most beautiful landscape I'd seen since leaving several weeks before. Living in Wales spoils you for holidays elsewhere.

All this natural perfection is of course under threat, because humanity in general and its bureaucratic sector in particular, whether out of envy or plain, brutal ignorance, cannot let well alone wherever the beautiful's concerned. There is a designated trunk road through the Lledr Valley, and trunk roads must, of course, conform to the requirements for width of carriageway, breadth of verge and the like. No matter that this road merely links the local with the local, or that its original designation had more to do with the now-defunct nuclear power station at Trawsfynydd, south of Ffestiniog, than with any logic of route. No matter that inspectors at public inquiries have strongly recommended that alternatives be canvassed and that nothing more than an environmentally sympathetic 'easing' of the current road be undertaken. It

OVERLEAF Afon Lledr, July. The Lledr is revered by fishermen as one of the great salmon rivers. The fish gather in deep pools below the rocky gorge by Rhiw Goch, to the mysterious recesses of which a rickety, private and adventurous fisherman's path dating from Victorian times gives access to the permitted.

must needs be brought up to standard, in a valley where nature has allowed no room for this. So rocky bluffs will be blasted away, their splintered remains buttressed with concrete, features such as the fascinatingly named roadside split boulder of *maen yr hen wraig sy'n melltithio* (stone of the old cursing woman) will be dispensed with, and the BMWs and jet-ski-towing four-wheel-drive vehicles bound for the coastal caravan parks of Ardudwy and Lleyn will whip through village and valley at regardless speed, perhaps giving those who clamoured in support of improvement cause for reflection and concern. Whether the balancing act between the conservation of land-scape which is an amenity for the whole of Britain, and the serving of regional interest can ever be achieved, is brought gravely into question in places like this.

The village of Dolwyddelan is pleasantly situated among meadows, the crook of a ridge thrown down from a shoulder of Moel Siabod providing shelter from the south-west wind that can funnel ferociously down the valley. The Roman road Sarn Helen, whose course winds as the landscape dictates from north to south – even the imperial geometries of Rome were defeated by the Welsh hills – forded the Lledr here before continuing down Cwm Penamnen and over to the Roman base at Tomen y Mur.

Cwm Penamnen, reached by the narrow, climbing road which passes Dolwyddelan station (on the miraculously surviving branch line connecting Blaenau Ffestiniog and Llandudno Junction), must have been a remarkably pretty place in former days. In its lower reaches the clear stream, which has run over gravelly beds where small brown trout dart, tumbles down to join the Afon Lledr in a sequence of pools and falls. On the east side of the valley the crags of Carreg Alltrem (High-looking Rock) give excellent and popular rock-climbing. But the valley's erstwhile light and open character hides under a sombre veil of spruce. Approaching maturity now, in a year or two the trees will be clear-felled and winter rains will denude the hillsides of soured earth, clouding the stream and rendering formerly viable agricultural land useless, disfigured and barren. Whether this is preferable to the other environmental disaster which faced Cwm Penamnen in recent times – the proposed pumped storage scheme, the ancillary works for which would have radically affected the character of the whole Lledr valley – is a moot point.

Penamnen in the late fifteenth century was home to Maredudd ap Ieuan ap Robert, who established a dynasty in these parts – the Wynn family of Gwydir, whom we'll encounter again in this chapter. The site of his house is easily found on the west side of the road and valley within the forestry plantation opposite Carreg Alltrem. It had fallen to ruin by the mid-nineteenth century, and its slates were used to re-roof the church of St Gwyddelan in Dolwyddelan. Built in the fifteenth century by Maredudd, the church is tiny, lapidary, and worth visiting. The old church had stood on the hill behind – Bryn y Bedd ('hill of the grave') – but as Maredudd's great-grandson Sir John Wynn (1553-1627) records in his *History of the Gwydir Family*, written sometime after 1580, it 'stood in a thickett, and he might be oppressed by his enemies on the suddaine in that woodie countery'.

This same concern for safety in a lawless country infested with bandits after Glyndŵr's rebellion and the Wars of the Roses must have dictated Maredudd's rebuilding work at Castell Dolwyddelan, a mile up the valley from the village. This imposing ruin owes its fine state of preservation not only to Maredudd, but to restoration work – or indeed romantic improvement – on the keep in the last century. It never was as it is now, but the image it presents, however inauthentic, is none the less grand, and the battlements are a wonderful viewpoint from which to watch cloud-shadow chasing across Moel Siabod, Dolwyddelan's mountain and one of the prime hills of Snowdonia. The castle was reputedly the birthplace, in 1173, of Llywelyn ap Iorwerth (Llywelyn 'Fawr' or 'the Great'), the brilliant military strategist and unifier of the northern Welsh throughout the early decades of the thirteenth century – but this too seems unlikely. Archaeological evidence suggests a later date for building on this site, when Llywelyn's campaigns had already established his authority here. The greater probability is that he was born at the old castle site, much lower down among the riverside meadows.

IOAN BOWEN REES

I join Ioan Bowen Rees, former Chief Executive of Gwynedd County Council and finest of writers in Welsh on our country's hills, for a walk. Patrician, unstuffy, approachable, this solidly built man of sixty or so with a shock of white hair talks about his Gregynog Press volume, *The Mountains of Wales,* the cheap edition of which costs a mere £185. One reviewer dismissed it sniffily on that account. When it came out a couple of years later in a cheaper-still edition from the University of Wales Press, Ioan answered the charge: 'The quib-ble about the Gregynog Press edition concerned its cost and consequent "elitism". I reject the idea that finely produced volumes cannot be justified. My mother collected several of these volumes at a time when, as a young teacher, she was having to help support her parents through the agricultural depression of the 1920s. Later, I met someone who had inherited Gregynog books from a collier father who had given up smoking to save for them, the better to endure the industrial recession in Pen-y-cae.'

He talks more about his mother. She went — first of her family to do so — to Coleg Prifysgol Gogledd Cymru, The University College of North Wales, to read Welsh and botany. There, she heard the first university lecture to be given in her own language, by the scholar Ifor Williams. She loved the literature of her own country and also loved its hills. Ioan tells me how sound she and his father were towards him when he was a child. When he complained of cold and hunger ('and I must often have done that!' he laughs), they would cajole him along. 'The first time that the hills became a pleasure rather than a pain for me was on the Bwlch y Rhiwgyr. As we arrived on top of the ridge, my father began to recite Keats's sonnet, "On First looking into Chapman's Homer", and there in front of us was that skyline of Lleyn over the water, stretching down to Ynys Enlli. There came a magic that day which these hills have never lost for me. I was under their spell.'

As we laboured up the abandoned inclines of Bryn Hafod y Wern quarries, Ioan talked about their history: of the Penrhyn lock-out at the turn of the century and the great labour leader W. J. Parry at whose behest in 1864 Hugh Derfel Hughes wrote for an eisteddfod competition his *Llawlyfr Carnedd Llywelyn*, the earliest published guidebook to a single mountain. I asked Ioan why the misconception lingered that the Welsh were a people ignorant of their own hills? 'Oh, I think that's quite simple. It's a matter of class, surely? The early mountaineers who stayed at the Penygwryd and such places didn't concern themselves with the activities of a lower class and the language in which they were expressed. They assumed pre-eminence for their own achievements.'

And Hugh Derfel Hughes, who was he? A miller's son from Llandderfel under the Berwyn, Ioan replied. He settled in Tregarth and became a weigher — quite a responsible job — in the Penrhyn quarry, and his grandson was the same Ifor

Williams whom Ioan's mother had heard deliver the first Welsh lecture in Bangor. Ioan went on to recite Hugh Derfel's description in the guidebook of being on the summit of Carnedd Llewelyn with the preacher Tanymarian in the January snow of 1864, watching the mist roll in beneath them; from that, he launched off into an account of how, in 1847, Tanymarian acted as guide and helper to Joseph Jukes in the course of his work in Wales for the Geological Survey, as a consequence of which both Tanymarian and Hugh Derfel became convinced evolutionists and Darwinians: 'So you see how fruitful,' he concluded, 'was the interplay between local knowledge and expert study in these hills even 150 years ago.'

He described another of Hugh Derfel's books, *Hynafiaethau Llandegai a Llanllechid*, published in 1866, in which are mentioned the *'hen meddygon cartrefol'* (literally 'old home doctors') swinging from horsehair ropes on the cliffs of Twll Du to gather plants there; Ioan swept on to talk about the shepherds, and Ifor Williams's recollection of a gathering on Bryn Eithin in the 1880s when his job was to follow the son of Bryn Eithin to the nape of the neck of the mountain, right behind the summit of Carnedd Llewelyn. When the lad was asked who had arranged for him to take up this allotted spot, he replied that he didn't know, only that the Bryn Eithin shepherd was to be there at daybreak on the morning of Helfa'r Braich, according to an old, old custom.

We reached the summit of our little peak. I thought of all the topics we'd ranged over and my mind ran back to words from one of Ioan's published essays: 'Now that we are all in danger of living suburban lives, wherever we dwell, there is some risk that the Welsh will lose what the mountains gave them, and that the mountains will lose their Welshness, and their whole inner environment of history, religion and art.'

I think not, so long as Ioan and his like exist.

Early in 1283, more than forty years after Llywelyn Fawr's death, and a few weeks after the death of his grandson Llywelyn ap Gruffydd (*ein llyw olaf*, 'our last leader'), the castle was taken by the forces — wearing white tunics in readiness for a winter campaign in the mountains — of Edward I, who repaired, strengthened and garrisoned it.

If it seems odd that so important a defensive work should occupy this apparently secluded position, then the convergence here of old lines of communication from the surrounding areas of Meirionnydd, Eifionydd, Arfon and Nant Conwy offers a simple explanation, as well as a network of attractive walks. The ancient trackway over to Nant Gwynant by way of the mires and blond moor-grass of the Bwlch Ehediad ('Skylark Col'; recent editions of the Ordnance Survey maps have changed this to the more prosaic Bwlch y Rhediad — 'pass of the slope') is particularly fine. It passes a memorial stone, beautifully lettered by the sculptor Jonah Jones, to those who died in a DC-3 aeroplane crash. The tailplane protruded for many years from a rather grim pool beneath the memorial, and I can remember hurrying past in my youth, as the shadows lengthened. The castle was then in the care of the Ministry of Works; you asked for the key for its padlocked keep from Bryntirion farm below, and I once left it unlocked to creep back and sleep here for an uneasy night when moonlight and my imagination figured forth many white-tunicked shapes on the bare wide floors.

Before we leave this valley of the Lledr, we should take a look at the house with the memorial column and slab on the other side of the road from the castle. This was the birthplace in 1796 of John Jones — John Jones Talysarn as he came to be known — the most celebrated and forceful Calvinistic Methodist preacher of the nineteenth century, whose biography by Owen Thomas is one of the great prose works of nineteenth-century Wales. A self-educated road-builder and quarryman, he evolved a new style of preaching where emphasis was on Christian conduct rather than doctrinal dispute. He still has disciples worldwide; the Reverend Ian Paisley, for example, has visited the house.

For those who follow instead the call of the high places, a traverse of Moel Siabod, whose *lion couchant* shape dominates the Lledr skyline, can be a memorable experience. A footpath branches off behind the castle to an old whetstone quarry, from where half a mile of steep, rough ground gains you the shore of what's marked on the map as Llyn y Foel, but which bears a far more poetical name too – Llyn Llygad yr Ych ('lake of the ox's eye'). Legend has it that the lake was formed when the eye of one of Hu Gadarn's oxen started out with the exertion of dragging the dreadful *afanc* from the Beaver Pool and fell here. The ridge that curves west of the lake to climb directly to the summit of Siabod is called Daear Ddu (Black Earth) – inaccurately for once, its rock being silvery and of a roughness the mountain scrambler will find sensual to tread. The long crest of the mountain, set slightly apart from the other peaks of Snowdonia, is one of the best places from which to view them and gain a sense of their complex topography. You can descend it past the old slate quarries at Rhos to the village of Capel Curig, a traditional haunt of the outdoor enthusiast, with the usual amenities – pubs, cafes, equipment shops, campsites, climbing walls and dry-ski slopes – necessary to that community's happiness. It's to my mind most notable as the birthplace of the field botanist Evan Roberts.

I knew Evan a little, and knew far more about him than that fleeting personal acquaintance might allow. You could not notice the moss campion, the rose-root, the alpine chickweed, the Snowdon lily or the purple saxifrage without his name springing to mind. He knew where they all grew, was accepted without dissent as the pre-eminent field botanist of his time, and as an ecologist of international significance. Both botany and ecology are formidably academic, yet this was a man who had ceased full-time education at fourteen. Evan was born in 1906, blind in one eye, his family very poor. He took his first job in the quarry at Rhos – hard, dangerous outdoor work which left him with the gasping lungs of the silicosis-sufferer. The bleakness, though, was not the whole story. There were the extempore intellectual and debating societies of the quarry *caban*, its tradition of self-improvement.

The story Evan loved to tell was of how, after a minor domestic row, his wife Mabel scolded him out of the house and from under her feet one bright May Saturday afternoon in the late 1920s. So he wandered up on Moel Siabod, where his eyes lit on a clump of purple flowers – *Saxifraga oppositifolia*, the purple saxifrage – among the grey rocks of the mountain. He didn't know what they were, but determined to find out, and so began one of the great sagas of passionate self-instruction. This chance encounter with an unknown flower led ultimately to his acceptance as *the* authority on the distribution of arctic-alpine flora in Britain.

Evan's encyclopaedic botanical knowledge obviously didn't come from academic sources – he had neither the means nor the time for access to those. Its tap-root reached into a reservoir of native lore that the science of botany had also relied on for its foundation – a lore which was passed down locally through the oral tradition, and which was strongly present in Evan's family. When his biography was published in 1987, it was called *Llyfr Rhedyn ei Daid* – 'his grandfather's fern book'.

After the closure of Rhos quarry in 1953, Evan was taken on as the first National Nature Reserve Warden of the Nature Conservancy Council. His special preserve was Cwm Idwal, and to be shown round this magnificent place by the old quarryman-botanist, with his strong hands and gentle, expressive voice, was a memorable experience. The students – and their professors – all came to consult and be instructed by him. The honours came too: Honorary MSc, MBE and, proudest of all, membership of the Gorsedd of Bards in 1975. He continued to lecture and lead students to his favourite locations in the mountains even into his eighties, by which time he was

---

The long valleys which sweep up from the coast to end beneath the high summits of the Carneddau are places of great calm and beauty, their peace undisturbed except by the raven's call and the quiet sheep of the hills. These are the best locations to see the herds of shaggy-maned wild ponies, small and hardy, which survive in these mountains.

stone-blind. After his death, a month before his 85th birthday in 1991, the local paper carried a simple headline: *'Mae Taid wedi mynd!'* (Grandfather's gone!) That was the measure of the affection and esteem in which he was held.

To rejoin the course of the Conwy from Capel Curig is a simple and pleasant matter. A path up the field opposite the post office takes you, by way of a brief stretch of native woodland behind the prominent rocky pinnacles, into the marshy valley of Nant y Geuallt. There are notable views back to Snowdon along Dyffryn Mymbyr, with its twin lakes, and in the bog which the path skirts you'll find the insectivorous sundew in profusion. After rising gently to a narrow col, the path drops down suddenly into Crafnant, which means 'valley of wild garlic', the presence of which is always a good sign of lime-rich and botanically interesting rock. Thirty-eight acres at the head of the valley are now a National Nature Reserve, fenced against the depredations of the ubiquitous sheep and sustaining robust growths of ash and hawthorn. The little crags of the reserve are festooned with a luxuriance of wood-vetch, and in early summer its rich cream and delicate purple flowering is a gorgeous sight.

Llyn Crafnant, a mile down the valley, is one of Snowdonia's prettier lakes, which makes it all the more sad that unsympathetic plantation, much of which has now been clear-felled, should have taken place on the slopes above. The alluvium washed into the lake by the streams which drain this slope is an obvious condemnation of short-termism in government forestry policy. In sites as sensitive and vulnerable as this, legislation should ensure that only selective felling takes place. The pity's all the greater as it's this hillside which fills the view from the pleasant lakeside cafe, where boats can be hired.

If your nerves need jangling again after the relaxation of rowing one of the boats around for an hour or two, then cross the ridge to the east to Crafnant's sister *llyn* of Geirionydd, which has for some years been a favoured haunt of those whose idea of pleasure is to disturb the quiet of the hills with power-boats towing water-skiers, or to race around on jet-skis. These activities don't take place at Crafnant because it's a reservoir and a good fishing lake. Geirionydd, ironically, is neither because of the high lead content from nearby abandoned mine workings; perhaps this fact explains something about those who find their 'sport' here.

Modern philistinism apart, Geirionydd does have two interesting cultural associations. The monument at the end of the lake is to Taliesin, along with Aneirin one of the two poets who stand at the very outset of Welsh literature in the sixth century, and about whom there is also a highly elaborate early Welsh folk-tale, *Hanes Taliesin* ('The Story of Taliesin'), in which he appears as child of the goddess Ceridwen. The group of twelve poems transcribed in an early fourteenth-century manuscript and attributed to him are thought by Sir Ifor Williams, the great authority on the period, to be the work of a native not of Gwynedd but of Powys, so Taliesin's association with this place is tenuous, based on little tradition and no established fact. But Geirionydd does at least figure in the bardic title of a very fine, though much later poet, Evan Evans ('Ieuan Glan Geirionydd'), who lived from 1795 to 1855. Innovative and versatile, his best work is part of the common stock of any cultured Welsh-speaking person. His finest poem is probably *'Ysgoldy Rhad Llanrwst'* ('The Free School House, Llanrwst') – a profound meditation, vibrant with detail, on time, youthful promise and the enduring power of memory. Several of his hymns, notably *'Glan Iorddonen'* and *'Beati Mortui'*, are perennially popular, in their stately simplicity of thought and utterance close to the spirit of Charles Wesley and Isaac Watts, and significantly better as poetry than their Victorian English counterparts.

Associations aside, it's a relief to leave Geirionydd behind and follow the lane down for a long mile to the church of Llanrhychwyn – one of the loveliest ecclesiastical sites in the region. Its greensward churchyard high above the valley of the Conwy lies among oakwoods and flowery meadows, out of which the ribbed rocks sweep up towards the high plateau of the Carneddau to the west. There are old yews, the ash and the mountain ash intertwine, voices of children at play drift up from the neighbouring farm. Inside the church is a wealth of pleasing, plain detail – local workmanship for the most part, in local materials. Its two naves are separated by crude, strong piers. The south aisle – the one you first enter – is the oldest part of the church. The door through which you came in is the same used by Llywelyn ap Iorwerth 800 years ago. The fabric of the rest of the building dates from the fifteenth and early sixteenth centuries, and may well be the work of our old friend from Dolwyddelan, Maredudd ap Ieuan. If so, then he must have been a man of taste and substance, for one of the treasures of this building is its coloured glass from that time, which was probably made in Chester. The robust humour and humanity of the faces depicted in its yellow stain, brown lines and faint greens – of Christ, St Mary, St John and St Rhychwyn – are so vital they seem almost contemporary, and they leaven the peace of the place with laughter.

Below us now runs the Afon Conwy, and it's time to return to Pont ar Gonwy by Llyn Conwy, from where we set out on this first circuit, and follow the river's course down. For six miles it runs north-east, gathering tributaries on its way, through a shallow moorland valley where birch grows plentifully to the attractive little stone upland village of Ysbyty Ifan, now mostly owned by the National Trust. *Ysbyty* means 'hospital' and, as its name implies, the village originally grew up around a hospice of the Order of the Knights of St John of Jerusalem, which was established here in 1189 to assist travellers crossing the wastelands beyond. On the Order's buildings and lands, the Princes of Gwynedd conferred privilege of sanctuary and other immunities from law. As a result, after the departure of the Order, the date of which is obscure, hospice and village became a haven for outlaws and in the

The fourteenth-century church of Caerhun stands within the
ramparts of the Roman fort of Canovium, which guarded the lowest
crossing of the Afon Conwy. Above the simple arch of the west door
is a crucifix tablet, its Christ-figure primitive, gaunt and affecting,
which dates from the time of the church's construction.

fifteenth century sustained a culture of lawlessness protected by surviving privileges and immunities. Sir John Wynn wrote that it had become 'a receptacle of thieves and murderers, who being safely warranted there by law...no place within twenty miles about was safe from their incursions and robbery'. Only when the long-departed Order was finally suppressed in Britain, and its lands confiscated – in 1540, as part of Henry VIII's dissolution of the monasteries – was this anomalous situation remedied in principle, though by then powerful local interests had, in practical vigilante fashion, taken matters into their own hands.

Today, you are hard-pressed to find any trace of this anarchic history. In its place, there is a neat estate village, its terraces bright with hanging baskets of *impatiens*, lobelia and trailing geraniums, circling round the elegant, twin-arched bridge – the sturdiness of the central cutwater buttress speaks eloquently of the force of water in spate. Garden plots with apple-trees and potato-patches slope down to the pebbly river from square-windowed, three-storey houses and smaller, square-dormered cottages with steep, pent roofs and tall chimneys. Flags bloom along the bank, the swallows are vociferous in flight, young women with infants in push-chairs stop to converse over tidy walls with older women in their gardens. The village shop is small and a little shabby; it still displays a chipped enamel sign advertising 'Woodbine – great little cigarettes'. The lollipop man outside the school is smiling and relaxed under his nautical cap. In places like this, it's possible to believe humanity has progressed since the fifteenth century.

Road follows river from Ysbyty Ifan down to Pentrefoelas, where the main A5 trunk road conducts the tourist down past the popular beauty spots of Conwy Falls and Fairy Glen to the ambiguous delights of Betws y Coed. If you find these less than irresistible, you may prefer to make for a different objective by following the minor road that heads north from the village to cross the A5 close by Pont Rhydlanfair. Take it in summer and you'll be wending your way between high, banked hedgerows with campion, stitchwort and the dog-rose in astonishing richness of multifarious pink flowering and with the purple moors beyond. The loveliest places are often the quietest and most unlikely. Pont Rhydlanfair itself is a high, elegant single-arch bridge, built at the architect's third attempt in 1780. Its parapet is often crowded with canoeists urging their companions on to exertions in the rapids below.

Beyond the bridge, and across the A5, the road climbs into an amiable country of hayfields, hangers of tall ash and oak, small whitewashed farm-houses and a deep-blue sky hazing pale over distant hills. Yet only a little way to the west, the landscape changes, becomes shaggy with outcropping rock; the dingles are now sedgey, bushed with rowan, birch and the sessile oak. Just at the transitional point is one of the great prehistoric landmarks of Eryri (Snowdonia) — the neolithic burial chamber of Capel Garmon, which dates from the third millennium before Christ. The archaeologist Frances Lynch writes that it is a monument completely in the Cotswold-Severn tradition which seems neither to have been influenced by, nor to have influenced, the other tombs in the Conwy area. Its builders seem to have been an isolated community in a rather inaccessible retreat, but one that offered fine upland limestone pasturage.

The site was excavated in 1927, but not much was found apart from fragments of Ebbsfleet and Beaker pottery. The narrow entrance passage, the chambers with their upright lining slabs, the huge capstone measuring per-haps three and a half by four metres above the western one, are all impressive in their way, but more resonant even than these is the sense of apartness the monument radiates. It looks out on to, but not into, the central massif of Eryri. As you stand on the great slab above the west chamber and turn your gaze from distant hills across the Conwy to the structure at your feet, you retain the same sense of looking on at, rather than into, the meaning and past

OVERLEAF Solitary amongst the hills, Llangelynin Old Church stands in its walled enclosure, the rock of the mountain shearing through greensward beneath which unknown numbers from throughout the centuries lie in their quiet graves.

life of the place. This detachment of outlook assumes a degree of necessity as you descend through the village of Capel Garmon (where the pub, the White Horse, is not to be missed) to Betws y Coed, a great place for the lover of wool-shops and museums.

Betws has a few fragments of interest. An inn-sign painted by the Victorian landscape artist David Cox is preserved over a fireplace in the foyer of the Royal Oak Hotel – the board is split and the colours dulled, but composition and execution of the two-foot-square work is vigorous, humorous and assured. And by the unprepossessing, ill-proportioned and poorly maintained fifteenth-century church Eglwys Fihangel (St Michael's) is a comically attractive little suspension bridge, which sways alarmingly as you walk across a slow, deep stretch of the river where large trout leap. It dates, surprisingly, from 1930, and offers a quick escape from town – though not, unfortunately, in the direction of Gwydir, which is our next point of interest downriver.

Gwydir Castle is sometimes open to the public, but if not it's no great cause for lament. Associative texture here is more rewarding than the actual sixteenth-century building, with which the Victorians interfered drastically. This was the home of Sir John Wynn, whose *History of the Gwydir Family* is one of the crucial texts for students of Welsh history; its glimpses into the life of the times it chronicles are by turns arrogant, uncouth, on occasion oddly magnanimous, but always bloody: 'This Thomas ap Robin was after beheaded near the castle of Conwy by the Lord Herbert for that he was a follower of the house of Lancaster, and his wife is reported to carry away his head in her apron.'

If you're looking for architectural glories, forget the castle and make your way instead up to the curious little Gothic chapel of Gwydir Uchaf, demurely positioned behind tall hedges next to the Gwydir Forestry offices, which themselves look to have been estate or almshouses. The building of the chapel in 1673 was the last notable act of the Wynn family of Gwydir. The stone is a pale ashlar, the chapel itself light and unusual, its wooden ceiling swarming with naive, rustic angels painted on a blue ground. The elaboration of the religious impulse here, by contrast with the simplicity of nearby Llanrhychwyn, is startling.

The village of Trefriw, piled steeply up the western slope of the Conwy valley, is a good place to start a circuit taking in four interesting lakes. The first of them, Llyn Cowlyd, is reached by a meandering track across the sky-lark-haunted moor called Cefn Cyfarwydd ('ridge of the story-teller'). The name suggests a connection with the oldest Welsh tale, *Culhwch ac Olwen*. In one episode, Culhwch and Arthur – the reference to him here is the earliest in British literature – consult the Owl of Cwm Cawlwyd, oldest and wisest creature after the eagle of Gwernabwy. The owl's response suggests that even at the time of the story's transcription, the forests evidenced by the bog-oak and rowan stumps that protrude from the peat of the valley bottoms were distant historical memory: 'When first I came hither, the great valley you see was a wooded glen, and a race of men came thereto and it was laid waste.' There is certainly no forest now at Cowlyd – just landscape at its most brutal and stark. Rough slopes slip into deep water (at sixty-eight metres this is the deepest of Snowdonia's lakes). Depopulation is the rule. Principal Rhys (John Rhys [1840-1915], philologist, folklorist and Principal of Jesus College, Oxford), collecting material for his magisterial study of Celtic folklore, was given a story relating to the old farm near the lake's dam. Fairies brought a baby here to be dressed, gave money, began to come habitually, and one day left behind some of the stuff they used in washing their children. The farm's serving-girl examined it and then touched her eye. When she went to Llanrwst fair next, she was surprised at the number of fairies there, some of whom she saw stealing cakes from a stand, at which she challenged them. They asked with which eye she saw them, she gestured, they rubbed it, and she never saw them again.

Llyn Eigiau, Cowlyd's northern neighbour to which it is connected by tunnel – part of a complex system of waterworks providing hydro-electric power to the aluminium works at Dolgarrog – has as a backdrop the impressive cliffs of Craig yr Ysfa. The reservoir's dam broke on a November night in

1925 – the fracture line is still obvious – inundating the village below with the loss of sixteen lives. The road that climbs up to it from Tal y Bont provides access to a fine skyline walk around the lake's head, but our immediate objective is just to the north, where the valley of Pant y Griafolen (Hollow of the Rowan Tree – a very common name in these hills, usually in places where none still grow) ascends to the louring and impressive corrie lakes of Dulyn and Melynllyn (Black Lake and Yellow Lake). The latter laps behind a moraine of impressive regularity, the former is obviously and oppressively deep. On the grassy spur east of Dulyn are hut-circles, cairns and field-systems which date from the Bronze Age, when a more amenable climate prevailed over what would then have been high, balmy pastures with thickets of rowan in the valley below. The track that descends gently back towards the Conwy, with glorious views, passes one of the most interesting prehistoric defensive sites in Wales, the Iron Age hill-fort of Pen y Gaer. Its position is striking, the ramparts particularly complex, but the most interesting and rare feature here is the *chevaux de frise*, an arrangement of stone spikes designed to break the momentum – and ankles – of attackers. It gives a charged insight into the precarious former life of this settlement.

A network of footpaths takes you down from Llanbedr y Cennin, the village below Pen y Gaer, to another site of exceptional historical interest in parkland low down by the tidal reaches of the river. This is Canovium, a Roman fort, probably built during Agricola's campaign of AD 77, strategically guarding the lowest crossing of the Conwy. Its ramparts are co-incident with the northern and eastern walls of the churchyard that occupies a little less than a quarter of the camp's groundplan, and they can clearly be followed by extension from the walls. The church is mostly fourteenth century

Conwy is the finest example of a walled-town-and-castle complex in Britain, built as part of Edward 1's campaign to subjugate Wales. The rectilinear street-plan is still obvious in this view, from the highest point of the walls on to the castle and the vital estuary-crossing which it commanded.

in origin. The simplicity of the west end is particularly attractive at evening, when the pink sandstone medieval crucifix tablet with its faceless, emaciated Christ, and the double bell-cot above, glow in the sun. The curlews call along the sand-flats; the tides pulse slow. In the graveyard one epitaph reads:

> In loving memory of Elizabeth, the dearly beloved wife of Gilbert Brown, aged 46 years. Also Betty, their beloved daughter, aged 4 years, Both of whom died at Dolgarrog on the night of November 2nd, 1925. Also The said Gilbert Brown Who died December 10, 1930, Aged 55 years. 'At rest'.

In this procession of churches down the Conwy valley we have left the best till last. Llangelynin Old Church lies almost 300 metres up among rocky bluffs on a shoulder of Tal y Fan. It dates from the twelfth century, but is essentially timeless, low and sturdy in its walled enclosure with the earth heaving and swelling against it. Inside, all is unerring simplicity. The north transept is a *Capel y Meibion* (men's chapel) – the sexes were segregated in local churches well into the nineteenth century. When I was last here, a mole had thrown up a mound of soil from between the flags of the floor. Painted on the east wall are Commandments and the Lord's Prayer in Welsh, proba-bly dating from the Restoration. In the churchyard, ash and hawthorn grow from a sheltering bank, the graves of the unnamed and the named mingle, the epitaphs on the latter expressing a sense of the place: 'There is much comfort in high hills'; 'Who shall dwell in thy holy hill?' The south-west corner has a well, Ffynnon Gelynin – a stone *cist* in a thick-walled enclosure, formerly roofed-over, which was supposed to have the power of divination. Clothes of sick children were placed in the water; if they floated, the child would live. It's scummy with algal growth and infested with pond-skaters now, nettles and ferns growing from its walls, the anxieties and miseries enacted here forgotten and unmarked by anything but the small, harebell-crested mounds of minimal record in which the churchyard abounds, and the significance of which is salutary to those who see here only peace.

From Llangelynin it is three gentle downhill miles to Conwy, the finest walled town in Britain and one of the great medieval sites in Europe. The castle and walls are extremely well-preserved; they are the late thirteenth-century work of James of St George, Edward I's Master of the King's Works in Wales. The best place to view the wonderfully integrated structure of the whole in its setting is from the western apex of the town walls, reached from Rosemary Lane. The temptation to compare the generally tacky and unkempt nature of the town, its ancillary attractions and interpretative apparatus with the way in which a comparable French *bastide* would be treated is both irresistible and, on reflection, depressing. If you wish to see Welsh tourism at its worst, linger for a while on the quay among the costumed Welsh ladies, mock galleons and souvenir stalls.

Better to clear out as fast as you can and race along the new coast road, by-passing – as time has done – the pleasantly seedy Edwardian seaside resorts of Penmaenmawr and Llanfairfechan, to arrive at Abergwyngregyn, in the valley above which is one of the most majestic sights of the Welsh mountains. This is Rhaeadr Fawr, one of the two finest Welsh waterfalls. To reach it you walk for a little over a mile up a good, gently rising path (halfway along which is an excellent small exhibition designed by the Countryside Council for Wales) through a beautiful valley where it's best for one's peace of mind to ignore the power lines that cross it. At its head you round a corner and there, in an amphitheatre of dark rock framed by wooded slopes, is the fall. It's more accurately a sequence of falls. The first, unseen in a wooded, rocky gorge above, feeds into a diagonal cataract which hits a pool at the top of the main cliff, which it jets over after turning sixty degrees. As it falls, bosses of black rock break it up so that when the water sluices on to the lower slab – seamed by diagonal cracks which have the effect of leading your eye into the

OVERLEAF The high tops of the Carneddau are the largest expanse of arctic tundra in these islands apart from the Cairngorm plateau. At a height of 1000 metres, these wastes of frost-shattered rock and club-mosses are far from any road, and serious country for the walker in winter.

scene – it cascades down in lacy patterns of a foamy whiteness that is in star-tling contrast to the underlying rock. The height of the whole is about fifty-two metres. People come, they sit on the boulders by the path, they gaze, stilled, as those do who enter the Taj Mahal. They watch the throb of the falling water quizzically, as though it imaged their own lives and then their attention drifts downstream, melancholy now, to where the pale-breasted dippers work among the rocks.

The valley above the falls, Cwm yr Afon Goch, is ancient and exquisite, leading up into the Carneddau. There's no wilder place in Snowdonia than the high tops of the Carneddau – for bare solitude they're matched in Britain only by the Cairngorm plateau. I remember being on the wide white dome of Carnedd Llewelyn – second highest of the Welsh peaks – one April afternoon. Wind had bitten into the crisp snow and etched sastrugi across its crystalline, untainted surface. Looking down the steepening slope to tiny Ffynnon Llyffant – at 850 metres the highest and most remote of Welsh lakes – I debated whether to unstrap my ice-axe from the sack, imagining the unstoppable slide, but indolence prevailed. The snow anyway was that perfect texture where a firm kick produces a secure toe-hold.

I soon arrived at the summit – alone, no one else on the hills, the sun westering but still high in the sky – and sat in the hollow cairn to eat an orange and ponder on the mystery of why people quit the hills so long before nightfall. It was six o'clock. An occasional bank of cloud encroached from the east, rolled across the moor and quickly dispersed. A bitter, subdued wind streamed constantly from the north. Peaks and snowy ridges radiated out in every direction. Below me, to give added sense of height, was the cliff that the eighteenth-century writer Thomas Pennant referred to as 'the most horrid precipice that thought can conceive'. The three prime hours of the day in terms of visual splendour were still to come, and yet there was not another person in view. I think people are frightened of these places, fright-ened of their solitude. Beyond the ice-crystalled walls of my shelter not a thing stirred but the wind. In a few short weeks the snow would have gone, melted. Dotterel, perhaps, would be scurrying in small flocks among the club-mosses and shattered stones of this bleak tundra. But for the moment it was a primal place, turning in the slow wheel of the day down towards darkness and marking its descent with magic.

The mountains at this hour begin to grow in stature, levered up by the slant of light. As I made my way slowly towards Foel Grach, Yr Elen was all bold monochromes of accentuated ridge and strata. At its back, Garnedd Elidir might have been the Dent Blanche. Ahead lay the five-mile ridge over Yr Aryg, Bera Bach and Drosgl down to Bethesda, and I wasn't going to hurry. These hills have an atmosphere unique to themselves. Even the detail – the frost-heaved surface, the scattered stone, the woolly profusion of moss and lichen – is different to that of any other part of Snowdonia. The feeling of the place is spacious, unvisited, unspoilt. I drifted on and found shelter among the rocks on the tor of Bera Bach.

The sun was a deep, orangey red, hanging over Holy Island, which was separated from the mainland of Anglesey by a glint of sea. As the sun sank into a dark band across the horizon, the peaks to my left glowed briefly, then became colourless and phantasmal. There was a flat period for a few minutes, until suddenly the sky on the horizon lit up and distinct bands of colour resolved from what had previously been neutral and obscure. Above me the sky was a dark blue, lightening imperceptibly to an eggshell-blue arc in the west which in its turn modulated into palest green and then a yellow streaked with dove-grey. Beneath this the bands were sharply defined: orange, a rosy mauve, muted purple and then charcoal grey above the glittering pewter strip that was the sea. And as if to balance this light-show in the sky, the red moor-grass all around me was leaping into vivid life. This spectral phenomenon always startles me and seems near-miraculous in its intimacy and close-at-handness, bringing in its evanescence an indelible sense of the mountain kingdom's power and glory, a sense which stayed with me as, in quiet exultation, I descended to the steep terraces of Bethesda.

CHAPTER TWO

BACKBONE

If you come to Snowdonia by public transport, the chances are that you will arrive in Bangor. Like Caernarfon and Conwy, the other two main towns of this northern coastal strip, Bangor has been adversely affected by road construction and municipal 'improvement' – though unlike them, Bangor doesn't have the saving grace of great medieval architecture to impose presence and atmosphere upon it. This is particularly unfortunate, given that it occupies a site of considerable antiquity. A *clâs* (monastic college) – one of many scattered along the coasts and throughout the hills of Gwynedd – was founded here around AD 525 by St Deiniol under the protection of Maelgwn Gwynedd. Within twenty years of the establishment of this early Celtic Christian foundation – the second oldest in the British Isles – the See of Bangor had originated. (The name 'Bangor' means a wattled enclosure, which is aptly descriptive of the original *clâs*. It occurs elsewhere at Bangor Is-Coed in the Welsh Marches, where Northumbrians massacred the monks of the Celtic monastery after the battle of Chester in 613, and at Bangor in Co. Down, another important monastic settlement.)

Why, apart from its age, this particular foundation – Bangor Fawr (Great Bangor) as it had come to be known by the early eighth century – should have taken precedence over every other in the region is a mystery whose answer remains locked into the history of the so-called Dark Ages. A

Rocks like sheaves of spears stacked for the wind's wars.

reasonable conjecture would be that it had to do with the character of Deiniol Wyn (Deiniol the Blessed). He was consecrated Bishop here by the important early church leader St Dyfrig (Dubricius), on the latter's retirement to Ynys Enlli in 546, and held office until he himself travelled west to Enlli and death at a date given in the *Annales Cambriae* as 584, but almost certainly twelve years before in 572 – the dates in early chronicles are notoriously unreliable. Deiniol left behind him bishopric, monastery and no doubt church, though nothing has survived of the two last. As Hughes and North write in *The Old Churches of Snowdonia*, the classic study of ecclesiastical architecture in Gwynedd, 'there is not a single original church founded by one of the early Celtic Saints remaining in Wales. Whether of wood or stone, all have disappeared and been replaced by later buildings, generally occupying the early sites.'

Unlike many of the other historical *clasau* in Gwynedd, very little remains here even of the physical site, and not much is known of it. Bangor would once have been very secluded. Seen from the sea, by which Deiniol would have arrived, the fault-valley through which the little Afon Adda (now entirely culverted) meandered between two steep and wooded ridges still impresses. In earlier centuries travellers here from the east had to contend with the traverse of Penmaenmawr, which even as late as 1774, when Dr Johnson came this way, inspired fear and anxiety. Those arriving from the west, as Giraldus Cambrensis did in 1188, found the going equally hard. In his *Journey Through Wales*, Giraldus recounts the fatigue occasioned in his party by descending Nant y Garth (the present-day B4547 road runs through it). At the bottom, Archbishop Baldwin sat on a fallen oak-tree and asked his fellow-travellers to whistle for him, but they were forestalled by a bird. A discussion ensued as to what type of bird; was it a woodpecker or a golden oriole? Someone mentioned that there are no nightingales in these parts, and the Archbishop joked that if the nightingale never came to Wales it must be very sensible, concluding: 'We are not quite so wise, for not only have we come here but we have traversed the whole country.'

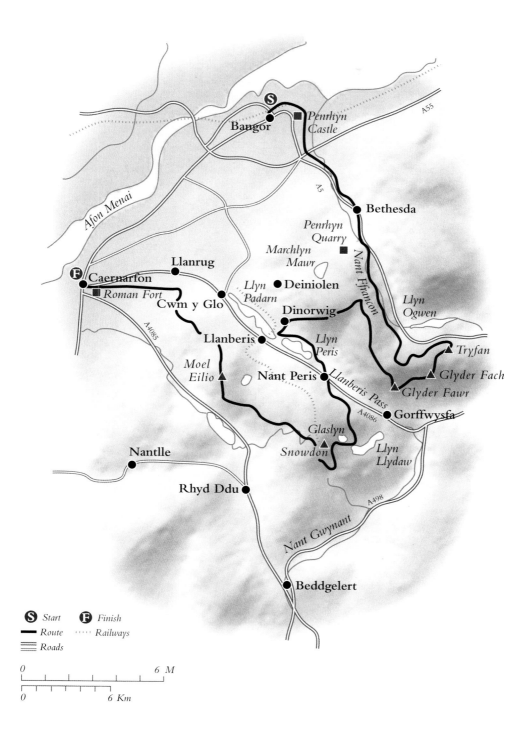

S

Penrhyn
Castle

Bangor

A5

Bethesda

Afon Menai

Penrhyn
Quarry

*Marchlyn
Mawr*

Llanrug

Nant Ffrancon

*Llyn
Ogwen*

F **Caernarfon**

Roman Fort

Cwm y Glo

*Llyn
Padarn*

● **Deiniolen**

Dinorwig

▲ *Tryfan*

Llanberis

*Llyn
Peris*

▲ *Glyder Fach*

*Moel
Eilio* ▲

Nant Peris

Llanberis Pass

▲ *Glyder Fawr*

A4085

A4086

● **Gorffwysfa**

Nantlle

Glaslyn

▲

*Llyn
Llydaw*

Snowdon

Rhyd Ddu ●

A498

Nant Gwynant

Beddgelert

S *Start* **F** *Finish*

—— *Route* ⋯⋯ *Railways*

≡ *Roads*

0   6 *M*

0   6 *Km*

The original church and enclosure here most probably occupied the same site as the present cathedral. During the recent construction of the Deiniol Centre, an early Christian cemetery was excavated, and seventy graves discovered where its car-park now stands. In the nineteenth century, many of Bangor's older buildings had early tombstones and other carved material incorporated into their fabric. One of the cathedral's great treasures, the Eva Stone, was itself found in 1879 among rubble under the wooden floor of the chapter house. Dating from perhaps 1380, it's a slab of fine-grained, light-coloured sandstone on which is cut in bas-relief and exceptional detail the figure of a woman. Even the pleats, plackets and eighty-five buttons down the front of her dress are represented. The cathedral itself, where the stone is on display, is disappointing both internally and externally. It is overlooked by a modern shopping centre, to make way for which the hotel in which Johnson stayed ('a very mean inn...I lay in a room, where the other bed had two men') was demolished in 1995. Inside, it's gloomy and ill-proportioned, and although its setting in remnants of the parkland that once surrounded the Bishop's Palace must have been attractive, all that changed when, earlier this century, the A5 trunk road was routed through the grounds and called – thunderbolts no doubt assailed the ears of the city fathers at this unwitting stroke of humour – Deiniol Road.

Its origins apart, Bangor's two main attractions are its university and its pier. The latter, newly restored to wrought-iron Victorian glory, stretches out across the Afon Menai almost to Anglesey, and in summer is bustling with buskers, fishermen, fortune-tellers, ice-cream vendors, rushing children, giggling pensioners, trippers and sun-bathing local winos. It is vital and well worth visiting. The university building at the top of the hill above the town,

PREVIOUS PAGES All the great valleys of Snowdonia lead out west into the sunset, framing the storm clouds and the fierce play of light which add to the drama of the Welsh mountains, the flat, comfortable lands of Anglesey beyond offering rich contrast to their ruggedness.

by contrast, is well worth *seeing*. In fact, you can scarcely fail to see it, it so dominates the town. It is a huge, robust, brown building, finished in 1911 and built from public subscription collected throughout North Wales. Old people in the area still call it Coleg y Chwarelwyr (the Quarrymen's College). It has a marvellous terrace at the front, and terraced gardens and quadrangles within. In itself, it is a wonderful piece of architecture, yet it is difficult not to lament for the lost opportunity here. Beneath Top College, as the old building is now called, there are slopes of grass and trees, hazed with bluebells in the spring. Across them have been built a students' union building that looks like a multi-storey car-park, a tawdry modern brick-and-steel theatre, and other high-rise academic buildings that cost significantly more than was anticipated because of the sodden underlying silts. If foresight, vision and appreciation of potential had been applied, something to enhance the beauty of setting could have evolved – college, cathedral and theatre as integrated whole on the flowered hillside, without dividing road, without ill-assorted, unplanned development. Could not Wales then, having capitalised on the prime asset that is its landscape, be proud? But if, as a nation, we are hard-pressed even to *conserve* what is beautiful, how shall we ever create it?

Leaving Bangor behind – without too many regrets – you soon come to an edifice that arouses in local people widely differing and ambivalent responses. This is Penrhyn Castle, mock-Norman and utterly grandiose, which was built between 1827 and 1847 for the Douglas-Pennant family. If the wealth the quarrymen freely gave enabled the construction of the University College, the wealth they created under hard and dangerous conditions of labour for the owners of the Penrhyn Quarry was squandered on

OVERLEAF The 300-metre high cliffs of Y Lliwedd, southernmost of Snowdonia's satellite peaks, were one of the earliest practice-grounds for the rock-climber. The West Buttress was climbed in January, 1883. Even before this date, Welsh copper-miners, lured by legends of King Arthur's gold, had ascended the severe cleft of Slanting Gully in the 1850s.

this posturing ostentation, which so brutally signifies the selfish primacy of economic power. There are many in Bethesda who still regard it as a symbol of oppression and exploitation. It is now, more happily and demotically, in the care of the National Trust, which has put a great deal of well-intentioned work into making it a major tourist attraction, with audio-tours, interpretation boards, tea-rooms, exhibitions, nature walks, adventure playgrounds, industrial railway museum and the like.

The growth of the great estates, along the sunny strip of the coast and away from the rough and windy mountains where the quarries which funded them lay, is an interesting area for study. The estate records, as they have been made publicly available, are often incomplete, and particularly so where they are relevant to the early period of their growth. It is clear, however, that a form of industrial and social blackmail, as well as the scandalous Enclosure Acts, contributed to the rapid expansion of these estates in the late eighteenth and early nineteenth centuries. Freeholders were offered employment in the quarries – a powerful inducement in a region where subsistence farming was the norm – on the condition that they exchanged their freehold for copyhold, which then reverted to the estate owner after two or three generations, the original owner's descendants becoming tenants at the landlord's whim (the same process is a theme in Hardy's novel, *The Woodlanders*). There is a local tradition that the house at the bottom of Nant y Garth around which the wall of the Vaynol estate performs two sharp bends was the property of someone who held out against this early form of industrial blackmail. The acquisition of estate lands by enclosure was equally unjust and ruthless, and led to riots, notably in 1808 and 1812, when common land on which cottagers had lived for many years was annexed, and the rights of those who lived there were deemed to be mere 'encroachments'. Once acquired, much of the land went for grouse moor, and in at least two cases protesters who had the temerity to act against the loss of their homes were brought to trial and, in order to provide an example, sentenced to death.

Folk memory of this process of coercion and wholesale theft, even among a residual community most of whose intellectual leaders have for a century at least been forced by economic necessity to emigrate, remains strong. In Bethesda, the quarrying town which is the next stop along our route, tactics used by the quarry-owners and managers in the bitter industrial disputes of the 1890s and early 1900s still, among the older people, give rise to vitriolic comment against the Douglas-Pennant family and Penrhyn Castle; to denunciation of those communities who provided blackleg labour to break solidarity in the great Penrhyn Quarry strikes of 1896-1897 and 1900-1903; and a generally expressed contempt for those who, in the damn-ing local idiom, 'took Lady Janet's cabbage' (i.e. accepted the parsimonious and conditional relief offered by the Castle 'Ladies' to families of those whom they deemed, on the word of informers in the community, to be the more deserving and less outspoken strikers). Graphic witness of this legacy of ill-will and mistrust is to be seen in fading graffiti on old walls here and there in the town, most often reiterating the word *bradwyr* – traitors!

Bethesda today is a fascinating and endearing community which has, like many of the old quarry towns, such as Penygroes or Blaenau Ffestiniog, managed to achieve a synthesis between the remnant industrial community which survived the demise of the quarries, and the incoming 'alternative' tribes, attracted by cheap house-prices, an extant post-industrial benefit cul-ture and the adjacency of magnificent landscape. So the streets are bright with coloured clothes, wholefood shops and 'healing centres' alongside the more traditional pub, Co-op and chapel. Indeed it was a chapel built in 1820 that gave the town its name. Before that it was a loose scatter of settlements across the lower ridges of the Carneddau: Gerlan, Llanllechid, Yr Achub, Carneddi, Cilfodan, Braichmelyn. The tourist bent on traditional beauty spots passes these places by and perhaps even considers them ugly. That is a shallow judgement. They have a character and resilience – in the shadow of the slate tips and across the reclaimed land of quarries like Pantdreiniog in the centre of the town – which is admirably and essentially Welsh.

DENISE WILLIAMS

By no stretch of the imagination could Dein-iolen be called pretty. The National Park boundary picks a fastidious line across the mountainside high above, in order to exclude. Shop after shop along the main street is empty, some of them approaching dereliction. You could be forgiven for thinking that this place does not have the feel of a thriving community. The bare statistics might bear you out. But call on Denise Williams, Secretary of Pentre Helen Tenants' Association, and you might, if you have any appreciation of human spirit in adversity, start to revise that estimate.

Pentre Helen is a council estate of a hundred houses, slung up across a few boggy fields at the bottom of the village in the 1930s and untouched since then. If you drive past on a still winter's morning, you see the smoke from the open coal grates, which provide the houses' only heating, rising up, mingling, hanging pall-like over the houses, the air acrid and sulphurous as a Dickensian fog. Lung problems and asthma are endemic. Maybe 75 per cent of the tenants here are unemployed, on low income, single parents. But it doesn't look like a place that's shrugged its shoulders and given in, defeated by circumstance. Open the neatly painted gate to Denise's tidy garden, sit down in her spotlessly clean, comfortable sitting room amidst the clutter of family pictures, start her talking and you know that here is someone who's keeping her dignity, fighting her corner in circumstances that would have the politicians and petty bureaucrats who allow this waste and human oppression grovelling.

She's been here ten years, has three young children – Daniella, Barry and Katie. Her husband's on one of the short-term, mask-the-true-scale-of-unemployment schemes which bring in £10 a week more than the dole. Barry, when he's strong enough, will need serious abdominal surgery at Alder Hey children's hospital in Liverpool. Denise will be there with him throughout, will sleep in the chair by his bed, not wanting him to be alone, frightened, without any English. He could have had the operation as a baby, she tells, but the doctor misdiagnosed, wouldn't listen to her, because mothers are just paranoid, aren't they? The doctor, not the mother, knows best. There's a wry composure as she relates all this, rocking Katie in her arms all the while. It's like the boundary drawn up there again, from which people look down – on Deiniolen, on mothers, on the unemployed, on the working class. 'Barry's not dumb,' she tells me, 'he's just had so many problems.'

And Denise's answer is not to take them lying down. She's red-haired, voluble, bright, and she's learning the techniques with which to fight for an improvement not just to the situation she and her family find themselves in, but for the estate as a whole. Through the Tenants' Participatory Advisory Service she and others on the estate learnt how to form a tenants' association. They are now networking with other estates, passing on tips, receiving advice, lobbying effectively even for simple things like a rubbish skip, but also for central heating, repairs, improvements to the houses, 200 metres up on a Welsh hillside in the face of the wind and the children sleep summer and winter in unheated bedrooms. The whole village needs an improvement scheme, a focus. There's so little money here. She recounts the discos, coffee-mornings, sponsored walks that raised money in the summer to take all the estate's kids to Y Rhyl for the day and give them £2 each spending money: 'It might not sound a lot, but for people on income support...'

She doesn't need to finish. She carries on to talk of the possibility of securing for the village a Rural Development Grant from the EC. She's an active part of a community which has every reason to be proud of its own efforts. Other places give in. Not Deiniolen. Its silver band's been the best in Wales four years running; Daniella's name is down for it. On the bus shelter at the top of the estate the graffiti reads *'Gwaith, Yr Iaith, Dyfodol'* (Work, the language, a future). Shame has no place here. It belongs with those who deny rights.

Beyond the huge heaps of spoil from the Penrhyn quarry, the mountains rear up, shapely and majestic presences with names that hint at wealth of stories: Carnedd y Filiast, Marchlyn Mawr, Cwm Llafar (Cairn of the Greyhound Bitch, Great Horse-lake, Valley of Laughter). The entire end of the valley leading south from Bethesda is stopped up by the mightiest wall of rock in Wales, which rears more than 750 metres from the foot of the Ogwen Falls to the summit of Glyder Fawr in little over the space of a mile. But before you leave Bethesda for the mountains, make sure of three things: that you sample the eccentricities of the Douglas Arms Hotel, opposite the ugly Victorian church of Glanogwen – a local institution where the landlord still charges for your beer in pounds, shillings and pence; that you walk in the woods of beech and oak alongside the Afon Ogwen, through which there are plans to drive a by-pass; and that, having seen Penrhyn Castle, you take a look at the terrace of Cae'r Berllan – at right angles to the A5 just beyond Austin Taylor's electrical factory – where, after noting the dimensions of the low, crog-loft cottages which housed families, you might well ponder the inequity between the living conditions of those who laboured to create wealth, and those born to it who, without sharing, enjoyed it.

Finally, though, we come to the mountains for which Arfon is famous. They lie in two parallel blocks of complex ridges, bounded to the north-east by Nant Ffrancon and Nant y Benglog, to the south-west by Nant Colwyn and Nant y Betws, and divided cleanly in two by a remarkable valley which was originally known as Nant y Mynach, but which is now invariably referred to as the Llanberis Pass. The mountains east of this divide present their most spectacular faces towards the curiously shallow lake, Llyn Ogwen – which, despite being over a mile long, is never more than three metres deep. From the car-park (in which there is a popular refreshment stall) between the mountain centre and youth hostel near the outflow from the lake, a path meanders gently for half a mile – as often as not under the feet of crocodiles of schoolchildren on geography field-trips – into Cwm Idwal, one of the prime sites for geomorphologial study in Britain. 'A house burnt down by fire did not tell its story more plainly than did this valley,' wrote Charles Darwin, though he went on to record that when he first came here in 1831 he did not notice 'the plainly scored rocks, the perched boulders, the lateral and terminal moraines' – all the evidence of the former presence of ice which has opened the eyes of countless students, instructed or self-taught, to the processes which shape landscape.

Cwm Idwal is one of the traditional haunts of the rock-climber in Snowdonia, and on most days of the year novices and the mellowly middle-aged can be seen scrabbling up the stripped and polished plane surfaces of the Idwal Slabs, on which most of the holds, from long usage and popularity, would adequately double as mirrors. The more forbidding ramparts of Clogwyn y Geifr (Cliff of the Goats) at the back of the cwm are commonly known as the Kitchen Cliffs, after the dark cleft of the Devil's Kitchen that splits them. The Welsh name for this feature, Twll Du (the Black Hole – in one or two local sources it is referred to as Twll Du Uffern, which translates more robustly as 'Hell's Arse'), is seldom used. The English name is anyway reputed to date back to the time when a party from a ship accompanying Edward I's campaigns was sent to discover the source of the clouds that so frequently bedevilled military operations in Eryri. They came across this chasm with the hiss of water and the vapour streaming out of it, and fled down the valley in terror, convinced that they'd stumbled across the chimney of the kitchen of the devil himself. The Kitchen Cliffs themselves are of variable interest to the rock-climber (although Menlove Edwards, the tragic figure who was the most radical of rock-climbing pioneers and finest of essayists on the sport, did make a bizarre series of ascents here). But they are of the utmost significance to the botanist, who finds on their lime-rich ledges a delectable variety of relict arctic-alpine flora. The obsessional nature of those who pursue this interest is fondly satirized by C. E. Montague in the much-anthologized story, 'In Hanging Garden Gully'. (For those wishing to take a closer look, this is the vertical feature on the extreme right of the cliff, and a 'severe' slime-and-grass climb.)

ABOVE Cwm Idwal, with its dark lake over which legend declares no bird will fly, is one of the classic sites for the study of geology in Britain. Charles Darwin first interpreted evidence for glaciation here: 'A house burnt down by fire did not tell its story more plainly than did this valley.'

LEFT Gorse and holly and crystal stream offer glittering relief from the cloud-draped greyness of the mountains above. In the proximities of rock touched with light or folded in mist lies something of the endless fascination of the Welsh hills.

The best route to the summits – the locality's chief attraction – is certainly the one which leaves the A5 from where the tenth milestone from Bangor formerly stood and climbs the North Ridge of Tryfan. The eastern aspect of this mountain is one of the most celebrated – and justly so – sights in our British hills, 'a small, Gothic cathedral of a mountain which seizes upon our imagination so as almost to exaggerate the effect of its own shapeliness.' Thomas Pennant, looking down on it from the Glyderau plateau to the south in 1781, described it as 'the singular mountain Trevaen, assuming on this side a pyramidal form, naked and very rugged.' His accompanying artist Moses Griffiths etched a romantically recognizable counterpoint to the words which is the child's vision of a perfect hill. And the Reverend William Bingley, two decades later, set the seal on a reputation for difficulty of ascent which has lasted to the present day by telling that he and his companion 'could scarcely take a dozen steps together in any place without at the same time using our hands.'

The two great natural obelisks that are the mountain's summit, when viewed from below along Nant y Benglog, so clearly give the impression of being gigantic standing figures that they have been known since the early nineteenth century as Adam and Eve. Bingley gives a suitably blood-curdling description of the antics of his companion, Peter Bailey Williams, Rector of Llanberis and Llanrug, upon them, and an interesting insight into attitudes of both visitors and natives at the end of the eighteenth century towards the Welsh mountains:

> The summit of Tryfan is crowned by two upright stones, twelve or fourteen feet in height, about a yard and a half asunder, and each somewhat more than a yard and a half across at the top. To stand upright on one of these, and look down the side of the mountain, would inspire even a tolerably stout heart with terror: to fall from hence would be inevitable destruction. But my companion stepped from the top of one to the other. I am not easily alarmed by passing among precipices, and my head is, I believe, as steady as that of most persons, but I must

confess I felt my blood chill with horror at an act that seemed to me so rash. The force necessary for the leap, without great management in its counteraction, would have sent him a step farther than he intended to have gone, would have sent him headlong down the precipice. He informed me that a female of an adjacent parish was celebrated for having often performed this daring leap.

The North Ridge is the most exciting route to the top of the mountain not to involve actual rock-climbing. In dry conditions, for those who enjoy rough, steep ground, the challenge is to take as direct a course as possible, teasing out throughout its length all the little problems: the clean walls of firm, silvery rock dappled with apple-green lichen, the blocky risings up which you consider your line before stretching your muscles upon it. In the first climbing guidebook to the Ogwen valley, published in 1910, J. M. Archer Thomson wrote of this mountain feature that 'on its broad crest, wayward humours and lively impulses may be indulged with impunity.' The ridge is a mountain feature of the highest quality, but the summit itself is a place apart. It feels sublimely aloof – more so, perhaps, than that of any peak in Britain other than those of the Black Cuillin in Skye. There is the fact that the road is only half a mile away, yet 600 metres beneath. There are higher hills all around, but none with Tryfan's stark simplicity of rock architecture. And there is the feeling too that, despite the numbers crowding the airy platform of the top, this is still nature's unadorned domain, its highest points those twin rock columns on the brink of the cliffs, to make the long stride between which, in mountaineering tradition, is to win the freedom of Tryfan.

OVERLEAF Crib Goch (red crest), a fretted blade of horizontal ridge high above the Llanberis Pass, is the first and most difficult passage in what many consider to be the finest mountain ridge circuit in mainland Britain – the Snowdon Horseshoe. An exciting scramble for the confident in summer, in winter it is terrain only for the well-equipped mountaineer.

The easy South Ridge of Tryfan gives a quick descent, the cwm of Bochlwyd with its lake and high, gleaming cliffs in front of you, to Bwlch Tryfan, through which the old miners' path – used by the men from Bethesda who worked the copper veins on Snowdon – threads its way before traversing screes to arrive on the ridge by Llyn Caseg Fraith. It seems that every mountain photographer who has ever visited Snowdonia has spent time sitting by this lake, hoping for the clear, windless, perfect day on which the rock-ribs of Tryfan's East Face are reflected across its unrippled surface. Most of them have to wait a long time before facing the dispiriting descent down the Miners' Path to Pen y Gwryd.

Although this path gives easy access to the summit ridge of the Glyderau, there is a much more satisfying line of ascent from Bwlch Tryfan, and one which, when taken in conjunction with Tryfan's North Ridge, provides the substance of one of the more satisfying mountain circuits in the British Isles. This is the Bristly Ridge; the Welsh name for this feature has apparently lapsed from local memory, but the English is precisely descriptive, for it does indeed bristle with rock spikes, spillikins and pinnacles. It gives an exciting scramble and prelude to the weirdest of all Welsh mountain tops – the summit plateau of Glyder Fach. At the end of the seventeenth century, the antiquary and botanist Edward Lhuyd, revising for republication William Camden's 1586 topographical work *Britannia*, visited the summit of Glyder Fach and described it thus:

> On the utmost top of the Glyder I observed prodigious heaps of stones, many of them of the largeness of Stonehenge, but of all the irregular shapes imaginable, and all lying around in such confusion as the ruins of any building can be supposed to do.

Towards the end of the next century, Thomas Pennant thought 'this mountain to have been a sort of wreck of nature, formed and flung up by some mighty internal convulsion.' In a sense Pennant was right, though the 'mighty internal convulsion' was only the slow, frost-shattering process of the ages. He went on to explain that it 'is covered with groupes of columnar stones of vast size, from ten to thirty feet long, lying in all directions.' A rock that particularly seized his attention 'was about twenty-five feet long and six feet broad. I climbed up, and on stamping it with my foot felt a strong tremulous motion from end to end.' Pennant's artist, Moses Griffiths, made a sketch of him on this rock – known today as the Cantilever – from which you might deduce that his employer was no more than three feet tall.

The great rock-garden plateau of Glyder Fach is not only a fascinating place in itself, its solid geometries hovering wonderfully on the brink of abstraction, 'dead bones of the eldest born of time' as Charles Kingsley called them; it is also absolutely central within the massif of Snowdonia's highest hills, and as such, provides as fine and panoramic mountain views as any point in Wales, stretching on clear days as far as Rhobell Fawr and Cadair Idris, thirty miles away to the south. Snowdon, too, presents its sharpest, most sculpted aspect in this direction. For those who like their hills wild, unspoilt and surrounded by other peaks, Glyder Fach should be their first objective. Come here on a summer's day when the clouds are broken and high, when the heather of the lower slopes is in mauve and purple bloom, and when Llyn Gwynant, 900 metres below, is a deep, clear aquamarine, and your heart will be lost to this landscape where time is an irrelevance, and where there is only stone and simplicity and wind.

It's an enchantment you should be wary of, for when the mist descends, a strange disorientation comes with it, shapes amplify, distort, and you need a compass to guide you from the magician's garden, lest you take the wrong one of many wandering paths. You head west, for example, to stop abruptly on the brink of the precipices which fall away into the Llanberis Pass from the spur of Esgair Felen. Another path strands you amidst the fierce coronet of Castell y Gwynt (the Wind Castle) – was there ever a more evocative name for a mountain feature? You can make your way down from the plateau by way of the ridge called Y Gribin back to Cwm Bochlwyd, but having striven to gain all this height and space, unless time's short it's infinitely preferable to carry on along the spine of hills which curves round to the north.

Glyder Fawr is the first of these hills. It is five metres higher than Glyder Fach, but so relatively undistinguished that Edward Lhuyd believed the latter to be 'utmost top of the Glyder'. Haskett Smith, the Victorian mountaineer, explained the difficulty well: 'Glyder Fach, though called "the lesser", is far finer than its brother peak, so that many have found difficulty in believing that the O.S. surveyors were right in ascribing seventeen feet of superiority to the more lumpy western summit.' He goes on to have fun with the name: 'Glyder – the meaning of the name is a mystery. One Welsh scholar gravely tells us that its real name is *clydar*, which at once yields the obviously suitable meaning of "a well-shaded ploughed ground".'

Haskett Smith and his fun aside, the derivation of 'Glyder', according to Ifor Williams, is from *cludair* – a heap of anything piled up together – which is certainly appropriate to Glyder Fach, less so to Glyder Fawr, from which you quickly descend to Llyn y Cŵn, the small lake nestling in the *bwlch*.

Writing in 1798, the Reverend John Evans – a Creationist whose observation of landscape was more acute than his interpretation of it – put forward the theory that at the time of Noah's flood a huge lake existed here, which by sheer weight of its volume sundered its restraining cliffs, thus forming the Devil's Kitchen and scattering their remnants across Cwm Idwal. Forty-four years later Charles Darwin reassessed the evidence and published his own views on the formation of Cwm Idwal, which were to prove seminal in the study of glaciation. The idea of there having been any large expanse of water up here is wonderfully far-fetched. Llyn y Cŵn itself is a windy little sheet of water abutting the steep scree of Glyder Fawr. In its

The visitor bent on recreation is often inclined to forget that Snowdonia is a working landscape, sheep-farming still an important, though declining, part of its economy even today. Here the shepherds get down to the back-breaking task of shearing in the Llanberis Pass, July.

brief summer, it is graced with bogbean and flowering lobelia; in its long winters with ice-flowers seeded on the rocks by the gale.

Beyond the lake, the ridge bends north, and a demoralizing slog brings you to the suave crest which bounds Nant Ffrancon to its west. All the way along beneath it there are text-book examples of glaciation: arêtes, moraines, cirques. These latter *cymoedd* – Cwm Clyd, Cwm Cywion, Cwm Coch, Cwm Bual, Cwm Perfedd, Cwm Graianog – grow increasingly impressive, the last of them having 300-metre glaciated slabs whose relatively easy angle is obvious only in profile. Pennant, in a fascinating aside in his *Tour Through Wales*, tells of local men informing him that 'if the fox in extreme danger takes over them [the slabs] in wet weather he falls down and perishes.' The precise observation recorded by that 'in wet weather' speaks volumes about local knowledge of these hills in past centuries. When the slabs are dry, a fox could pad down them at the limit of friction. In the wet, as the anecdote records, they become a death-slide.

At Carnedd y Filiast, above Cwm Graianog, the ridge's final spur plunges down towards Penrhyn Quarry, once reckoned the largest man-made hole in the world and still working today, albeit on much reduced scale. From up here, the play of light across this *diminuendo* of hill-ridges, their descent to moor and plain, their opening to sea and sunset, is often of startling beauty. A last summit lies off to the west, above what Patrick Monkhouse described in the 1930s in his vivid *On Foot in North Wales* – one of the best walking guides ever written – as 'the least-known of the first-class Welsh cwms'. Both cwm and summit have a grievance to be expressed for them against colonial attitudes. The latter appears on the map as 'Elidir Fawr', a name first imposed on it in 1842 by the Ordnance Survey and which has no foundation in Welsh. It, and the equally imperialist imposition of 'Elidir Fach' on to the hill-which-is-no-hill known locally as Braich Melynwyn, were coined simply to balance out Glyderau Fawr and Fach at the other end of the ridge. The proper Welsh name, which ought to be reinstated, is Carnedd Elidyr, in commemoration of Elidyr Mwynfawr, son-in-law to Maelgwn Gwynedd.

The proximity of Marchlyn Mawr (Great Horse-lake) also supports this name; Elidyr was mentioned in the very early Welsh texts, the *Trioedd y Meirch* (Triads of the Horses), which were transcribed in the earliest extant Welsh manuscript, the *Llyfr Du Caerfyrddin* (Black Book of Carmarthen). In this account, Elidyr's horse, on which he arrived from the Old North (the Welsh-speaking regions of northern England and southern Scotland), could carry seven and a half persons: himself, his wife, five followers and a jester who ran at the side and held on to the crupper, thus making up the half-person. True and false names apart, the gritty rocks of the summit shelter-cairn look out both on the bronzed sandflats of Traeth Lafan (desperately polluted with heavy metals and radiation from Sellafield, according to a recent Friends of the Earth report), and on the shining sea to the west.

The 'least-known of the first-class Welsh cwms' that lies beneath Carnedd Elidyr's summit has an even more tragic tale to tell. Adding to the presence of the place is a legend related last century by a quarryman, Evan Lloyd Jones of Dinorwig. A farmer's boy, rescuing a trapped sheep, stumbled across a cavern in the cliffs. He entered and saw on a table the crown of Arthur. When he stretched out his hand for it, the cave darkened and filled with thunder, causing the boy to flee. The lake below was now foaming with waves, and he saw there a coracle, in which were three peerlessly beautiful women attended by a rower. 'The dread aspect of him that rowed was enough to send thrills of horror through the strongest of men...no health remained in his constitution after that, the mere mention of Marchlyn enough to make him insane.'

There is in fact a system of rift passages in the very striking Craig Cwrwgl (Coracle Cliff) above Marchlyn, which men from Dinorwig explored with ropes from the quarries last century, but where they found no treasure. A more poignant story, however, and one which offers an interesting insight into the activities of local landowners at the time of the Enclosure Acts, was collected by Principal Rhys in Dinorwig in the 1880s:

Sam Roberts and I walk up the Miners' Track on Snowdon and he talks as we go, filling in his own background detail: adventurous Caernarfon boy going out at nights into the bay in the bows of his father's boat; early love of the mountains ('Of course I first went up Snowdon in wellies in winter – didn't we all? And of course that affects how I talk to people. If I see a couple of kids setting out like that, I'll give them all the help and advice I can. If I see a teacher dressed in all the latest gear leading an inadequately clad school party, I'll make no secret of what I think should be done there either.'); local Welsh boy starting to climb; Liverpool University, which he left after a year, drifting in and out of jobs. Eventually – after a lift with two soldiers who promised their life had everything – he signed on for nine years in the Royal Marines: 'There were good things about it, but at the end I was on the streets in Belfast and that's no job for a soldier. But before that there were things like the Arctic Warfare School in Norway. They taught you to ski, sent you into the wilderness with an eighty-pound pack, and I remember returning from one exercise down twenty miles of hard-iced track. Even without the pack you needed to be good just to stay upright. So I lashed the skis to the pack and sledged, ran into the C.O. lower down and got two days' restricted privileges and a report saying I was unfit for mountain warfare. When my nine years were up, they tempted me to stay with an Everest expedition, but the same C.O. was the leader so I left.'

Sam has been a National Park Warden now for twenty-three years, and has been to Everest three times — most recently on a crazy scheme to paraglide from the top. At the end of the trip he wrote home:

'Greetings from Katmandu
The mountain this time we could not do
The wind too strong
The air too cold
And perhaps I'm just too bleeding old.'

But it's this mountain, Snowdon, which is his home country and he knows it intimately. As we pass the mine barracks by Llyn Teyrn, he mentions that they were used only for a few months and were abandoned as being too damp. I ask where he learnt that. 'From John Morgan, who used to work at the Britannia Mine. He lived at Blaen y Nant, and died ten years ago, in his nineties I think. His job was sorting the ore as it came out of the adits, so that spoil heap down to the left of the zig-zags is probably his work in the main. Stone on stone...'

By the Llydaw causeway, three youths, surly, walk towards us, ghetto-blaster thudding disco-beat across green water.

'Excuse me, would you mind turning the music down. It affects other people's enjoyment.' The request is ignored, repeated, complied with. 'The volume'll be back up the minute they're round the corner,' he shrugs ruefully.

A little farther on by Glaslyn we meet an Asian family, trainer-shod, summer-clothed. They quiz Sam on time, distance, terrain, ask whether they'll make the top.

'It's half past four now. It'll take you at least an hour, possibly more, to the summit. It's dark by eight and the forecast's for rain. Stick together, give it a go, but make sure you're turning round and heading down by six, six thirty at the latest. So long as you're back down here by dark you'll come to no harm — and you'll have an adventure.'

The group's buoyed up and, under his careful direction, starts to scramble up the initial rocks. He shoots me a sidelong, conspiratorial, approving glance, a smile spreading over the lined, wise face.

We head down. He tells me about a new warden who's been appointed for the Carneddau.

'I suppose there was a flood of applications from gimlet-eyed careerists with impeccably typed CVs and ecology degrees from the Central University of Newcastle-upon-Tyne?'

'There was,' he replies, 'and the job went to a young lad who's worked on the hill farms for the last ten years since he left school at sixteen. He'll do well.'

About seventy years ago, when the gentry were robbing the poor of these districts of their houses and of the lands which the latter had enclosed out of the commons, an old woman called Siân William of the Garnedd was obliged to flee from her house with her baby – the latter was known later in life as the Reverend Robert Ellis, of Ysgoldy – in her arms. It was in one of the Marchlyn caves that she found refuge for a day and a night.

The caves of Marchlyn would have afforded poor and savage shelter for ageing mother and baby. And barbaric as the treatment of the poor was in the last century, so has been the treatment of the land in this. Marchlyn Mawr is now the top lake for the Dinorwig Pumped Storage scheme: its dam is enlarged, its shoreline is tidemarked, noticed, prohibited, and its peace and beauty utterly destroyed. When the Central Electricity Generating Board toured a publicity caravan round the local quarrying villages to tout for approval for the scheme in the 1970s, it claimed, over a life-size photograph of Lulu displaying her cleavage, that the scheme would lead to better television reception in the area, that it would employ almost exclusively local labour in its construction, and that it would respect the proud industrial legacy of the quarrymen. In retrospect, all three statements look dubious, and the main purpose of this economic white elephant is to provide a surge of power into the national grid at times when the nation switches on its kettles for tea at the end of some popular television programme.

From the top of Carnedd Elidyr you can descend only about 100 metres to arrive on the top levels of the Dinorwig Quarry, whose castellated spoil-heaps, inclines and abandoned workings tower up for 600 metres above Llyn Peris. Unlike its counterpart above Bethesda, Llanberis's quarry, after two centuries of continuous production, closed in 1969. At the height of the industry, in 1882, its output was 87,429 tons of slates and it employed 2757 men. By 1968, the number of employees had fallen to 300, and the next year a major rock-fall – the pale spill of rubble from which is still clearly visible near the top of the workings – took out the roadways, electrics and hydraulics to the levels still in production, at the same time as a number of debentures became payable by the operating company. The place was sold, and shortly afterwards sold on again at a profit of reputedly staggering proportions — insider dealing was not a term which enjoyed any currency twenty-five years ago — to the CEGB as the site for its Dinorwig Pumped Storage scheme, the effect of which on the upper lake of Marchlyn Mawr has already been related.

As a piece of industrial architecture, Dinorwig is monumental, its scale beggaring belief. There is an excellent museum dedicated to the slate industry in Wales at Gilfach Ddu, by the lakeside; the oakwoods of Allt Wen have been designated a country park, and the ruined landscape around Allt Ddu and Pant Sardis extensively landscaped with the help of EU grant-aid. But it is the quarry itself which draws you in. Even on luminous days, I find it oppressive. In the gloom of a November afternoon it becomes unbearable. The men whose brief, hard lives were spent wresting from the mountain the rock from which were split rank upon rank of headstones in Deiniolen cemetery under which they now lie, had life expectancies significantly and measurably shorter than those who did not work in the industry. In Blaenau Ffestiniog in 1875, the average age at death of men who had not worked in the quarries was sixty-seven; for those who had it was thirty-seven. They carved their choked lives' monuments, creating others' wealth. Search out for yourselves the old Anglesey Barracks where workers lived during the week, by the *llwybr o gam i gam* (zigzag path) down to Llanberis, and witness the conditions there.

The slate itself is curiously beautiful. When I travel by train from Wales to London, I beguile the last few miles into Euston by identifying the source-

OVERLEAF A Blondin — named after the Victorian tight-rope walker — lies on the grass whilst another sags on its rusting wire amidst the forlorn grandeur of the Dinorwig slate quarries. The closure of these quarries came about in 1969, the result of massive rock-fall, a pale spill of scree from which is obvious on the left of this photograph.

quarry for the slate roofs of the houses by the line. There is a whole range of turquoise and purples in a rock slandered by the description of being merely grey. The sun highlights fold and fracture, bodies them forth as shapes that you realize with a sudden shock were the defining geometries of quarry-men's lives. Where one *bargen* (section of rock allotted by management to a group of quarrymen) is regular and true, another is splintered and bent — nature's accidents dictating even the sufficiency of a child's daily bread. But all that is finished now. Lacy brilliance of parsley fern colonizes gaunt tips, the tiny stonecrop spreads bulbous and globular among razor litter of the terraces, rosettes of lichen encrust and emboss. A pair of choughs tumble and scream. Scratched initials from the last century hide shyly in the darkness of tunnels. There are trees rooting everywhere; a tenacious birch sapling trem-bles on a cliff-ledge, sycamores obscure the angles of an incline, and an ash tree grows by the old *caban*, a shed where the quarrymen took their breaks.

I know it was a *caban* because Rennell Pritchard of Dinorwig, who worked here years ago, told me so before his death. Not that there's much left of it now. The slates from the roof, the table and the workmen's rough benches were taken long since. The lime render is flaking and loose, nettles grow in the hearth and the inevitable spleenwort sprouts from the walls. I'm struck always by how small the *caban* is: three by four metres, no more than that. The small window looking out on to Snowdon and the lake is frameless, glassless now, and the door's gone. Yet the place still breathes, even whispers. If I stood here in November on a day when the mist muffles every sound and is so dull that even the generator hum which now permeates this mountain is deadened, I think that the old echoes would creep back warily to the place which gave them birth. There would be voices here again. As I stand here now, a quarter-century after the quarry's closure, perhaps 100 years beyond the *caban*'s time, I see paragliders circling on thermals like garish raptors with their prey dangling; on rock slabs, climbers — with whom the old workings have become popular — in vivid pastels pad and poise, delicate-footed where the facemen's hobnails sparked. This roofless room draws me away from that modern and modish world to the preoccupations of another time.

What would the men have talked about? In the archives of the University College in Bangor there is the minute-book of a turn-of-the-century *caban*. It is entitled *Llyfr Cofnodion hen giniawdy Sinc y Mynydd, Llechwedd*, and it runs from St Valentine's Day 1902 to mid-April 1905. I don't imagine that the workers of Llechwedd were significantly more or less intelligent than their counterparts at Dinorwig. I suppose the topics raised in one month, October 1902, are pretty much representative of the thoughts, the interests, the mind-set and the mind-play, of workmen in the slate industry at the time.

There's singing – either serious solos, or more playfully the musical contortionism of setting the words of *O Fryniau Caersalem* to the tune of *Crug-y-bar*. There's recitation – of a poem that had been read only twice, and of an abbreviated *Dafydd Brenin Israel*. There are competitions on grammatical themes – read a passage from which all the punctuation had been removed, spell difficult words, create new ones. There are discussions – should ministers of religion have a lifetime's or a defined term's appointment to office; should the measures of the 1902 Education Act as they affect Wales be opposed; is the taking of a wife a matter of choice, or a necessity? There are lectures too – 'How much greater is a man than a sheep' runs the title of one; in another, Owen Morris talks about his holidays. All this took place in dank tunnels, in crude huts 600 metres up a mountain, in rain and wind, as the men slaked their thirst with bottles of cold tea and ate probably no more than dry bread. Yet, does that range of subjects, that desire to play and perform, that involvement with the issues of the day, that eagerness to live the

OVERLEAF Wales's grandstand! From the summit of Snowdon, a string of blue lakes, their water coloured by copper in the rocks, leads the eye out east, and teases the imagination with story and intriguing historical fact. The most visited mountain top in Britain, it has its railway to thank for that unenviable status.

life of the mind hold sway in works canteens today? Was the breadth, the awareness, the pride evinced through those activities an expression of the men's proud knowledge of difference, of cultural resistance, of intrinsic superiority to the vain, philistine and greedy proprietors who allowed them so meagre a living?

I look across the abandoned terraces to where the rock-climber moves up a bald slab. Out of adversity is produced elegance and grace, moving with a purpose, reaching a goal. In the jumble of scree beneath, pipework which drove the cutting machines is twisted as though it were cardboard tubing. The walls totter, the inclines sag wearily, their work done. At their head, the wooden drums are scored deep by the hauling wire. One day, the buttresses which hold their axles will collapse and, freed, they will bound crashing down into the encroaching oakwoods, from which rises the green wood-peckers' crazed laughter. These are haunted places, and the contrast between here and the tourist bustle of Llanberis is too great for me to stomach, so I shall lead you away along the old footpath that passes the quarry holes – hundreds of metres deep – of Matilda and Victoria to slip away between tongues of waste into fields and down to the old church at Nant Peris.

In high summer this is a beautiful place, basking in the glory of its setting. Above the riverside meadows are velvety green oakwoods and glinting rock outcrops on the lower slopes of the hills, which rear up on every side and lead your eye to the distant red screes and spiky crests of Glyder Fawr and Crib Goch. The jagged triple peak of Tryfan – Snowdon has its own version under this name – soars above the belfry of the medieval church, which stretches out long and low, sheltered by a thicket of ash and yew from the winter's blasts. The churchyard itself is a secret place, one of nettles and long grass and jackdaws calling from the ash trees. It's set back from the road. You enter it through a rough, lop-sided lich-gate. Barns with rusting corru-gated iron roofs crowd its perimeter and the graves huddle together in little clusters among the hummocks and clearings. They are almost all of the local Dinorwig slate, muted purple speckled with greeny-blue ovals like two-dimensional thrushes' eggs. The hierarchies are wonderfully displaced. In this, his last abode, the miner of 6 Rock Terrace rubs skeletal shoulders with the quarry manager of Hafodty, and the former occupants of Tŷ'n yr Aelgarth lie side by side with those of Tai Newyddion.

There are two graves here between which passes a certain frisson. One of them is a squat slab which lies against the church itself. Its inscription reads: 'Underneath lie the remains of William Williams, upwards of 25 years botanical guide at the Royal Victoria Hotel, who was killed by a fall from Clogwyn y Garnedd, June 13, 1861, whilst pursuing his favourite vocation. This tombstone was erected to his memory by a few friends.' Twenty metres away, on the other side of the path and between two yew trees, is a large, flat slab, whose ornate lettering recounts the following story: 'Sacred to the memory of the Reverend Henry Willington Starr, B.A., Curate of All Saints, Northampton, who perished on Snowdon while on a tour through North Wales, September 15, 1846, aged 32 years. And whose remains, discovered June 1, 1847, were interred beneath this stone June 7, 1847.'

The connection between the two men is a watch, and it remains a puzzle. Let me tell you first what is known of the last days of the Reverend Starr. He arrived in Caernarfon in the afternoon of 14 September, found lodgings in Pool Street, and the next day, 15 September – the day on which, according to his tombstone, he perished – he travelled on to Llanberis, where he spent the night in the Dolbadarn Hotel. On Wednesday 16 September, a misty day, he left in the morning to climb Snowdon. His name did not appear in the visitors' book at the summit. His carpet bag and great coat were not collected from the Pool Street lodgings where he had left them. There were two reports – not contradictory, but certainly odd – of sightings of him at Cwellyn on the Tuesday, and descending from the Glyderau on the Wednesday evening. Thereafter, silence. Searches were initiated and rewards offered, but without success. Until, on 1 June the following year, a solitary huntsman combing the ground beneath Clogwyn Llechwedd Llo on the flank of Moel y Cynghorion to the south of Llanberis found a red shawl, which the landlady of the Dolbadarn Hotel recognized as the Reverend Starr's. It then became known that his knapsack had been found a month previously. The next day the huntsman and the landlady's son-in-law returned to where the shawl had been found, to search further; it didn't take them long to discover what remained of the Reverend Starr. An inquest was opened, the remains identified, and William Williams was one of the witnesses called.

He surrendered to the authorities a watch identified as Starr's which he claimed to have found on the morning of 2 June, after hearing of the discovery of the shawl. The watch was rust-free and in perfect working order, which seemed remarkable in view of Williams's claim that it had lain out on a mountainside for the duration of a Welsh winter. He was reprimanded by the coroner for conduct likely to create suspicion of his integrity. The stories he used to explain finding the watch changed over the years. The unspoken suggestions aroused by the incident hung heavy over a community becoming increasingly dependent on the new industry of tourism. Williams himself disappeared on a fine June day fourteen years later. The Sunday before he had attended service at Capel Jerusalem, Llanberis, and had put half-a-crown − in those days, a considerable sum in this community − into the collection plate for a poor widow. The following morning he conducted two visitors to Snowdon's summit; he was to guide them down to Beddgelert but, leaving them briefly to botanize, did not reappear. His body was found days later at the foot of one of the treacherous gullies on Clogwyn y Garnedd, to which he had gone to pick rare alpine ferns for his many clients in that time of mania for their collection. The end of a broken rope hung down the steep section of the gully. There is no mystery about the death of 'Wil Boots', as he was known at the Victoria Hotel where he worked. He was simply, as his gravestone tells, 'pursuing his favourite vocation'. But he took with him to his grave who knows how much of the truth about the fate of his fellow victim, the vigorous and rather old curate from the boot-makers' capital who is now his fellow sleeper.

There is another, even more tragic tale to be told before we quit Nant Peris churchyard, and it concerns little John Closs, seven-year-old son of Robert Closs, landlord of the inn at Nant Peris. John was staying with his grandmother (five miles away) in Betws Garmon, on the west side of Snowdon, where his mother used to walk to visit him from time to time. On the afternoon of 17 December 1805, not wanting to be left behind, he decided to follow his mother back over the mountain to Nant Peris, not telling his grandmother of his plan. It was snowing; his mother's tracks were covered and he lost his way. His body was found three days later, high up by the summit of Moel Eilio, crouched and frozen in the snow. The epitaph on his tombstone was composed by the poet Dafydd Ddu Eryri, the great sustainer of bardic tradition in the area at the turn of the nineteenth century.

From Nant Peris, the pass — one of the finest and wildest in Britain — winds up to Gorffwysfa Peris, where there is a youth hostel (the old mountaineers' inn of Pen y Pass), car-park and cafe, as well as the starting point for three of the routes up Snowdon. Just below the bridge of Pont y Gromlech, where the road steepens for its final climb, is a group of enormous boulders which reputedly fell out of the great corner in the columnar cliff above (this is Cenotaph Corner, one of the most famous of Welsh rock-climbs, first ascended by Joe Brown in 1952). A particularly gruesome monster, the child-devouring hag called *Canthrig Bwt*, reputedly had her home under these. The people from the nearby farms knew of her, their children feared her, but it was not thought that she did them any harm. Or not, that is, until a day came when a workman sitting by the rocks noticed his dog eating something. It was a child's hand, and a missing finger identified it as that of a boy who had recently gone missing. The hag was lured out from beneath her rock and her head was struck off. Nowadays climbing babes, regardless of the grim history, disport themselves on the stones with practised and comfortable ease. And so we arrive at Snowdon.

I have a recollection of an experience on Snowdon which is perhaps the most precious of all my hill-memories. It is of walking up through the drizzle of a pre-dawn into cloud-filled Cwm Glas, plodding heavily on enveloped in mist, with no hint of anything other than more of this suffocating stuff to come, until suddenly, at Bwlch Coch, I burst into a clearer world. How to describe a beauty so ephemeral you were witness both to the moment of its existence and its passing? Its component parts were a pale blue sky, a white cloud-sea shading to rose in the east, shadowed blue slopes of island peaks, still air, and two points of movement across the whole scene: from Bwlch y Saethau opposite, pink cloud frothed in a slow fall; on the ridge of Crib y Ddysgl above a fox flicked his brush, glanced down towards where I stood, and in a glisten of rich chestnut was unconcernedly gone.

I do not take it as entirely gratuitous that this happened on Snowdon, for this is the most magical of British mountains. Its quality has nothing to do with height – Ben Nevis and Scafell Pike, high points of their respective nations, are mere lumps – but everything to do with architectonic structure and a quality George Borrow sensed: 'It is from its connection with romance that Snowdon derives its chief interest.' Physical form, association, myth and a long history of human awareness mingle cloudily about Snowdon and distil into the most heady and potent of mountain brews. It is a mountain whose dimensions we can approach from an extraordinary number of directions: the stilled folding of its rocks; the rich flora left behind after the retreat of the ice; folk-tale echoes of an older race; the unexplored archaeology of stone circle, hut circle, cairn; chronicled time, industry, sport. On all these levels, Snowdon has something to give to the effort of our understanding. Borrow was only half-right in asserting that connection with romance, for the legends that attach to Snowdon are earlier than that, are a crucial part of the source material for late-medieval European romance. Yr Wyddfa, Bwlch

---

The Afon Glaslyn, in its brief course, flows through four lakes and a gorge of exceptional beauty. Here, in its infancy, it spills down from the slopes of Snowdon through a ravine – on the shady walls of which grow many rare species of fern – to meander peacefully through the meadows of Nant Gwynant.

y Saethau, Mur Marianau, Cwm Tregalan, Llyn Du'r Arddu – these names remind us that there is perhaps a greater accretion of myth and legend upon Snowdon than on any other British hill.

Take, for example, the complex of tales concerning Merlin's appearance at Dinas Emrys and the last battle between Arthur and Mordred in Cwm Tregalan, which almost certainly pre-date their French and English chivalric counterparts. They are securely rooted in precise physical context. The account given by the eighth-century monk Nennius in his *Historia Brittonum* of the emergence of Merlin as wizard, beneath its wonders and elaborations, fits with astonishing exactitude both the physical detail of its location (at Dinas Emrys, above Beddgelert), historical fact, and archaeological evidence from the site. The Arthurian stories, with less supporting evidence, still locate here with equal precision. Arthur is at Dinas Emrys when word comes to him that Mordred and an army of Saxons are at Tregalan (the Town of the Enemy), below Bwlch y Saethau (Pass of the Arrows). Avoiding ambush in the narrows of Cwm Llan, Arthur marches over Bwlch Cwm Llan to surprise them and drive them back to Bwlch y Saethau, where, in the moment of victory, he receives his fatal wound.

In alternative endings, Arthur is either buried here under a cairn, Carnedd Arthur, which was recorded as still present in 1850, or – in a version of a story told also about El Cid, Frederick Barbarossa and Owain Llawgoch – he sleeps with his knights in a cave on Lliwedd, awaiting the call to arms (see also the Marchlyn story above). The apparent cave in Slanting Gully on Lliwedd was traditionally known as Ogof Arthur, and so strong was its lure that in the 1860s miners from Nant Gwynant ascended it, hoping to find Arthur's gold (or perhaps, more prosaically, rich lodes of copper). When, forty years later (by which time the gully had gained a huge reputation for difficulty and witnessed at least one fatality), a pair of English adventurers climbed it and, in true colonialist fashion, claimed it as their own invention – what, after all, did the Welsh know about their native hills? – they discovered in the middle of the most difficult section a rusting miners' stemple (an iron spike driven into the rock) from the true first ascent. Today, the feature is a 300 metre 'Severe' rock-climb.

As for later accretions to the Arthurian legend, it's probable that Tennyson had Llyn Llydaw, below Lliwedd, in mind in *Idylls of the King*, in scenes such as that when Bedivere, 'stepping down/By zigzag paths and juts of pointed rock,/Came on the shining levels of the lake.' Or again, in Arthur's departure:

> Dry clash'd his harness in the icy caves
> And barren chasms, and all to left and right
> The bare black cliff clang'd round him as he based
> His feet on juts of slippery crag that rang
> Sharp smitten with the dint of armed heels –
> And on a sudden, lo! The level lake
> And the long glories of the winter moon.

The scene of Arthur's passing over to Avalon ('Avilion' in the poem) in a barge attended by three queens was lent added poignancy by the discovery, almost contemporary with the poem's publication, of a dug-out craft in Llyn Llydaw, revealed when the lake level was lowered to facilitate mining operations.

A folk-tale which perhaps pre-dates even the Arthurian material attaches to Llyn Du'r Arddu (Black Lake of the Black Height) on Snowdon's northern flank beneath Clogwyn Du'r Arddu, the most magnificent of all British rock-faces. A fairy woman comes out of the lake, marries a mortal, brings cattle as her dowry, is struck by iron three times unwittingly, and at the third blow returns with her cattle into the lake. The story has parallels throughout the Celtic realms, many scholars believe its basis to be in conflict between Bronze Age settlers and Iron Age invaders, and in this instance cite in evidence the proximity of Bronze Age settlement in Cwm Brwynog.

All these resonances add a vibrant dimension to a peak whose physical presence is majestic. The structure and balance of its ridges, cwms and summits are strikingly grand from most angles. Even George Borrow, normally so unresponsive to mountain scenery, directed on it his stately praise: 'As for the Wyddfa [Snowdon's summit] I now beheld it high above me in the north-east looking very grand indeed, shining like a silver helmet whilst catching the glories of the setting sun.' Wordsworth, as he leads into the conclusion of his great philosophical poem *The Prelude*, chooses an incident which took place not on his native Cumbrian fells but here on the Bwlch Main ridge of Snowdon, which he visited on a walking tour in 1791:

> ...a Light upon the turf
> Fell like a flash: I look'd about, and lo!
> The Moon stood naked in the Heavens, at height
> Immense above my head, and on the shore
> I found myself of a huge sea of mist,
> Which, meek and silent, rested at my feet:
> A hundred hills their dusky backs upheaved
> All over this still Ocean, and beyond,
> Far, far beyond, the vapours shot themselves,
> In headlands, tongues, and promontory shapes
> Into the Sea, the real Sea, that seem'd
> To dwindle and give up its majesty,
> Usurp'd upon as far as sight could reach.

It's an odd thought that at the time of Wordsworth's visit Snowdon was rapidly becoming established as an important venue for copper-mining. Open-cut working at the top of Cwm Merch probably began in the seventeenth century, and the Reverend William Bingley, in the account of his tour

The imposing final peak of Snowdon, Yr Wyddfa (the burial place), towers above the coppery-blue lake of Glaslyn. In old Welsh stories and poems, the summit cairn was said to be burial mound of a legendary giant, with whom Arthur came into conflict in the earliest reference to him in British literature.

in 1798, mentions mining operations that had commenced a few years previously at Glaslyn. Production of copper ore ceased on Snowdon only in
1916. The early climbing pioneers on Lliwedd – the epicentre of mountaineering achievement in Britain in the era before the Great War – would
have had to contend with the cacophonous noise from stamping mills in the
cwm beneath. The mines, once abandoned, gave rise to their own folklore.
The Snowdon mine by Glaslyn and the Clogwyn mine east of Clogwyn
Du'r Arddu have consistently been rumoured to connect, and the direct distance between their openings is little more than a quarter of a mile. The
rumour has never been confirmed, and is thought unlikely to be true. A similar modern underworld myth was told by Mrs Williams of Halfway House,
the ramshackle and invaluable refreshment hut which used to stand on the
Llanberis Path to the summit (it was blown down in a gale, and the National
Park authority has taken a particularly dog-in-the-manger attitude towards
the reconstruction of this valid and traditional example of local enterprise).
In Mrs Williams' account, two children disappeared from Nant Peris in 1934
after going to play in one of the lakeside mines. They were found four days
later wandering around Llyn Du'r Arddu and, she added, 'it was reported
in the paper'. No doubt the date on it was 1 April. The Snowdon miners
certainly made some valuable contributions to the mountain's amenities over
the years. The first refreshment hut at the summit was put up in 1837 by
Morris Williams, a miner; the tracks to Clogwyn Du'r Arddu, Glaslyn,
Cwm Merch, Cwm Llan, and the one from Snowdon Ranger were all built
by miners.

   As the pressure on Snowdon this century has increased, its effect on the
fabric of the mountain has become more and more obvious. We can no
longer be so sanguine as Geoffrey Winthrop Young when, between the wars,
he exhorted us to 'Look forward fifty tens, and fifty more' years, commenting
that 'Other the boys, other their transient fame,/Snowdon will look the
same.' Nowadays, the freedom of the hills is increasingly seen as coincident
with responsibility towards their conservation (in some perceived state of

nature which may never have been, and certainly was never static), so our interest in them has to be represented by management schemes and bureau-crat-babble: 'Restoring Snowdon to an appearance which befits its international status and to enable the mountain to withstand the sort of pressures which are being put upon it (and are likely to be put upon it in the future) will depend largely on the success of management schemes designed to meet and overcome the demands made by its very popularity.'

Let's climb our mountain. That a hill which at the latest survey can muster only 1085 metres (3559 feet) above sea level (if surveys are to be trusted, it's apparently sunk between three and four metres this century) should have six major paths of ascent as well as innumerable variations says much about its metaphysical as well as its physical stature. It is possible to ascend Snowdon from Llanberis on the mountain railway, as hundreds of thousands have done since it opened at Easter 1896 (briefly, in the first instance; a locomotive left the track on the descent, and a passenger was killed when, in panic, he leapt from his carriage). It's a very exciting ride, though you have to endure the craning proximity of fellow-passengers, much dangerous wielding of video-cameras, and if you have a large family a second mortgage will be necessary to cover the fares. I prefer to walk, and the only problems with which you are faced are those of choice. The Miners' Track, closely followed by the Pig Track, are the most popular, and both start from Gorffwysfa car-park, the height of ascent therefore being significantly less than by other routes. They join above Glaslyn to ascend the zig-zags to Bwlch Glas. In winter – which on Snowdon can be any time from October to May – this last slope frequently banks out with ice, and is an accident black spot. In summer it's merely a traffic black spot. The

OVERLEAF Clogwyn Du'r Arddu, on Snowdon's northern flank, has long been celebrated by rock-climbers as the finest of British cliffs. Amongst botanists, who made the first recorded climb here as long ago as 1798, it has been venerated over centuries for the rarity and beauty of its relict arctic-alpine flora.

Llanberis Path is, like the town from which it sets out, deeply dull, and unconscionable since the demise of Halfway House. Its only use is to rock-climbers and botanists bound for Clogwyn Du'r Arddu, where in 1798 Bingley and the Reverend Peter Bailey Williams made the first recorded climb in Wales with their ascent of the Eastern Terrace:

> Mr. Williams, having a strong pair of shoes with nails in them, which would hold their footing better than mine, requested to make the first attempt, and after some difficulty he succeeded. When he had fixed himself securely to a part of the rock, he took off his belt, and holding it firmly by one end, gave the other to me: I laid hold, and, with a little aid from the stones, fairly pulled myself up by it. After this we got on pretty well, and in about an hour and a quarter from the commencement of our labour, we found ourselves on the brow of this dreadful precipice, and in possession of all the plants we expected to find.

The western flanks of the mountain give two rather better lines of ascent. The Snowdon Ranger Path meanders pleasantly through a lake-dappled cwm before beginning the serious business of ascent; it is the oldest of these paths, and has a splendidly open outlook. The Beddgelert Path, which these days starts, confusingly, from Rhyd Ddu, has equally fine views and a sharp, dramatic ridge in its upper reaches. The Watkin Path, from Nant Gwynant, is enclosed for most of its length, and the top section is the vilest and loosest ground on Snowdon. The facilities of the summit hotel – a slabby concrete shed designed, if that's the word, by Clough Williams-Ellis – become vital after climbing this. Any evidence at the summit for the burial place (*Wyddfa*) of the legendary Rhita Gawr (Rhita the Giant) has long since been subsumed in generations of re-modelling.

This leaves us with two circuits and a descent. The 'Snowdon Horse-shoe', which starts and finishes at Gorffwysfa, is, with the North Ridge of Tryfan/Bristly Ridge/Y Gribin circuit, one of the two finest British mountain traverses outside Skye. It needs a steady head in good weather, and mountaineering proficiency in winter. The southern horseshoe, which takes the old mine-track — an idyllic and beautifully engineered green path through stands of Scots pine — into Cwm Merch, climbs up the back of Lliwedd, endures the top section of the Watkin Path and descends the Bwlch Main ridge, is always quiet, and the best itinerary from Nant Gwynant. As for descent, the long ridge over Clogwyn Du'r Arddu and the successive summits of Moel y Cynghorion, Foel Goch, Moel Eilio and Cefn Ddu, with the sea always in front of you, is much the most attractive prospect.

From the end of the ridge you can diverge by way of the hamlet of Bryngwyn to Llanrug old church — some buildings are ruined by time, others by their restorers — in the burial-ground of which lies the Reverend Peter Bailey Williams, friend and companion to many of the early travellers to Snowdonia and foremost among a group of clergyman-scholars known as 'yr offeiriaid llêngar' (the learned priests), whose efforts helped preserve much of the poetry, tradition and purity of language in Wales at the turn of the nineteenth century. Alongside the church, an avenued track with ivy, campion and bryony along its verges links in to a sequence of footpaths through secretive country with hips and haws and fine, tall hedgerow trees, standing stones on knolls, brief glimpses of light on water at Abermenai, meadowsweet, explosions of pigeons' wings, shadowed hills behind against pale, sunlit slopes, copses of alder, the curlew and the lapwing calling. This lush, contrasted land leads down to Caeathro and Caernarfon, from where the next stage of our journey starts.

CHAPTER THREE

HEARTLAND

Of the two great walled towns of Snowdonia, Conwy may be the better preserved gateway to the region, but it is Caernarfon that stands indomitably at the hub of the heartland. Comparisons as to which is the finer are unilluminating. They are beyond question the outstanding walled-town-and-castle complexes in Britain. For most of the year their siege by tourists goes unrelieved. They are both Royal Boroughs, chartered by Edward I in the autumn of 1284, following the war of 1282–83 in which Llywelyn ap Gruffydd, the last native Prince of Wales, had been killed at the Irfon Bridge and his brother Dafydd hanged, drawn and quartered at Shrewsbury Cross. But here the similarities end; in character, the towns are vastly different.

Conwy, its castle squat and resistant on a rock with the orderly, enclosed, rectilinear little town behind, has contracted a virus, a superficial rash of holiday trivia from the anglicized resorts to the east, and its dignity suffers thereby. Caernarfon, a designated World Heritage Site, is more determinedly downbeat, yet at the same time more atmospheric and impressive – a workaday little grey town of the west rubbing shoulders unconcernedly with the magnificence history has bestowed on its site. Welsh (with the occasional summer burst of German, American or Japanese) is still the language of its streets. The market on Y Maes, under the upraised statuary finger of Lloyd George, Earl of Dwyfor and erstwhile Member of Parliament for 'Carnarvon

Cloud shadows dapple the western ridges of Snowdon.

Boroughs', continues to flourish where Edward once projected to take his ease among gardens. On Friday and Saturday nights the tribespeople down from the hills still whoop and carouse about the streets as wildly as ever did the Ordovices, the native tribe of this region 2000 years ago.

In one of the most famous and vivid descriptions from Classical history, Tacitus recorded in his *Annals* how, in AD 60, Suetonius Paulinus and his legion crossed the Afon Menai a mile or so east of Caernarfon to mount an attack on Anglesey:

> The enemy was arrayed along the opposite shore in a massive, dense and heavily-armed line of battle, but it was a strangely mixed one. Women, dressed in black like the Furies, were thrusting their way about in it, their hair let down and streaming, and they were brandishing flaming torches. Around the enemy host were Druids, uttering prayers and curses, flinging their arms towards the sky. The Roman troops stopped short in their tracks as if their limbs were paralysed...In the end exhortations from their commander and an exchange among themselves of encouragement not to be scared of a womanish and fanatic army broke the spell. They overran those who resisted them and cast them into their own flames, and destroyed the groves sacred to savage superstitions. (These people regarded it as a right to sprinkle their altars with the blood of their prisoners and to consult the wishes of the gods by examining the entrails of humans.)

The assault by Suetonius on territory reputed a stronghold of British resistance was little more than a piece of characteristically bloody military opportunism and derring-do by a commander who was looking continually over his shoulder at rivals, rebellions and recall to Rome. When the last had discreetly taken place, prompted by Suetonius' draconian behaviour after the defeat of Boudicca and his inept governance, the Ordovices of Gwynedd enjoyed an unruly period of grace, massacring Roman cavalry units and otherwise asserting themselves until in AD 79 a second campaign against them by a greater commander, Agricola, ensured their subjugation (or indeed near-

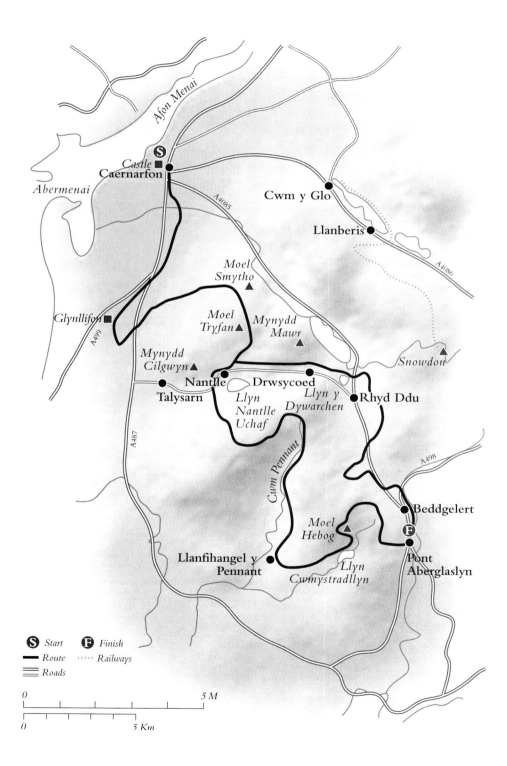

annihilation, for their settlements hereabouts did not recover for 200 years). Agricola was concerned not to repeat the mistakes of his predecessor; he knew the negative impact of a continued reign of terror and the necessity for just and efficient provincial government. It was in pursuit of the latter, as well as in the assertion of his military capability, that he established the major Roman base in North Wales, probably in the latter part of AD 79. This was the fort of Segontium, a hard and tense day's march across the Roman road through Bwlch y Ddeufaen from the camp at Caerhun, which we visited in a previous chapter; it is one of the most fascinating and complete Roman sites in Britain, its history reflecting that of the Roman occupation over more than three centuries.

Segontium's excavated foundations are clearly laid out to view on a flat table of land by the Beddgelert road, looking down on town and bay, with a little museum at hand to interpret them to the visitor, and a west wind whistling through the Scots pines. Far fewer people come here than to the castle below, yet it is in its way at least as redolent a site. There is evidence of other Roman usage clustering round it: a temple of Mithras in the dell behind the church of Peblig (a Welsh version of Publicius, reputedly a son of Magnus Maximus, whom we'll come to in a moment); a tile-kiln where a subway crosses under the flyover, which the stupidity of so-called planners inflicted on the town in the 1970s; and the solid masonry of Hen Waliau (Old Walls), a marine store incongruously incorporated into modern development by the Pwllheli Road.

Interesting though all this fragmented factual text may be, Segontium's deep fascination lies in the dimension where history resolves into legend or even myth, and thus exercises its influence over later events.

Finest of all prehistoric Welsh hill-forts, Tre'r Ceiri (town of giants) reveals within its massive drystone fortifications up to 150 hut-circles which archaeologists have shown were inhabited in some cases well into Roman times. The walls and gateways are in excellent condition, thanks to the work of the Gwynedd Archaeological Trust.

There survives, in a Welsh manuscript from the first quarter of the fourteenth century, a story – obviously much older – called *Breudwyt Maxen Wledic* (The Dream of the Ruler Macsen). It's a curious, tight-knit tale with a glowing simplicity. Macsen, Emperor of Rome, falls asleep whilst out hunting; he dreams of a beautiful maiden and in the moment of anticipated possession awakes inconsolable except by finding her. He sends out messengers to the furthest parts of the world to look for her, they find their way to Eryri, 'the rugged land which our lord saw', and in a castle at the mouth of the River Seint – the modern name is Seiont – they discover her, Elen Lueddog (Elen of the Hosts) as she becomes known. (The text mentions as the point of departure for their sea-crossing 'a great city at the mouth of a river, and in the city a great castle, and great towers of various colours on the castle', which is an accurate contemporary description of Caernarfon, perhaps implying that the *cyfarwyddion* – the itinerant story-tellers who maintained the oral tradition in medieval Wales – were still active and incorporating new material into their tales at the beginning of the fourteenth century. Conversely, and less likely, there is the teasing possibility of Edward or his master of works having been specifically acquainted with the story and modelling their works upon it.) Macsen comes to marry Elen, bestowing on her father as bride-price the Island of Britain to be held under Rome. He dallies, is deposed, and returns with his brothers-in-law who retake the city and restore him to its throne.

A sequence of historical facts seems to underly this fiction, which came down, no doubt significantly modified along the way, through 900 years of oral tradition to the time of its transcription. In about AD 382, a Roman commander in Britain of Spanish descent called Magnus Maximus won a significant military victory over invading Picts and Scots. In 383, he invaded Gaul: one of his generals caught and killed the emperor Gratian, senior Augustus in the west, and Maximus thus held Britain, Gaul and Spain. In 387, he crossed the Alps, an action that soon brought him into open conflict with the emperor Theodosius, who controlled the central and eastern empire, and on 28 July 388 Maximus was captured and killed at the battle of Aquileia. Beyond that, there are a few intriguing scraps of historical record: that a unit called *Seguntienses*, undoubtedly raised in Caernarfon, was serving in Illyricum, to the south-east of Aquileia, during or slightly after this period. The same source suggests by default that Segontium was abandoned by 380 or 390. In the mid-sixth century the monk Gildas, in his habitual moral demolition of early rulers, accused Maximus of opening the flood-gates to barbarism through his absence; Nennius, 250 years later, referred to him in similar terms.

Whatever the facts, this story seized upon the Welsh imagination with peculiar force. Many modern historians have located in it the genesis of Welsh nationhood. Gwyn Alf Williams, always provocative and exciting, states that 'Wales is born in AD 383 with Macsen Wledig', and having woken you up with a challenge, qualifies himself by adding that 'this is a Wales of the mind, created much later'. In the case of the mythical Macsen – for we have discarded now the defeated and alien Maximus – the recurrent motif in Welsh history of needy present nationhood revising for its own purposes dim or sparse historical fact asserts itself in the time of the second dynasty of Gwynedd, when royal genealogists set to validating their rulers by establishing a line of succession from him. By a fanciful conflation of Elen Lueddog with St Helen, they managed to bring in even Constantine the Great, the first Christian Emperor of Rome. Through that connection, after Edward I's defeat of the House of Gwynedd in the war of 1282–83 we are back with Caernarfon's other great historical monument, its formidable castle.

There is a substantially argued theory that this magisterial building was, at Edward's request, specifically designed by James of St George, Master of the King's Works in Wales, to evoke Constantinople and thus assert the mythical Constantinian association. It was certainly a part of Edward's project in the establishment of his authority to subsume Welsh heroic myth into his own regal identity. Another Welsh text dating from the time of the castle's construction, *Breudwyt Rhonabwy* (Rhonabwy's Dream), is very revealing here. Its anonymous author, writing in the court of the last independent Welsh dynasty, that of Powys, bitingly satirized Edward's comprehensive appropriation of and identification with the Welsh hero Arthur, by presenting that usually revered figure as a muddled and incompetent fool, inferior in strategy and intellect to a leader from the Welsh heroic age in the Old North, Owain ap Urien.

But this was a satire from a nation on the brink of mergence. The historical reality lay in the extraordinary architecture of Caernarfon Castle, by turns fantastic, as in the triple-turreted Eagle Tower, and brutally powerful, as in the banding of grey limestone masonry with brown sandstone, which emphasizes the bulk, extent and impregnability of this outstanding edifice among the finest series of medieval buildings in Britain. Fflint, Rhuddlan, Conwy, Cricieth, Harlech, Beaumaris, Caernarfon – symbols of oppression they certainly were (to some still are, as opposition to the investiture of the Prince of Wales here in 1969 proved), but their overwhelming presence is magnificent. Not that this proved entirely effective during the protracted process of their building. One revolt in particular, against punitive taxation in 1294–95, resulted in serious damage to the half-built Caernarfon Castle and the hanging, drawing and quartering of the Sheriff of Anglesey, in mimetic revenge for the deaths a dozen years before of Llywelyn and Dafydd, whose skulls were still mockingly impaled on pikes within the Tower of London. The rebellion was put down by Edward with his usual savagery, and work on the castle, which did not cease until 1330, recommenced.

The old town of Caernarfon lies within the circuit of the walls (private houses and buildings abut these in distinctly medieval manner, so for the most part they are inaccessible), which are complete apart from a gap of perhaps ten metres where the Green Gate once stood. It's an attractive place, though the atmosphere is much diminished by the development of an extensive council administrative block. The award-winning mock-Swisseries of this are already beginning to look gimcrack and jaded. What remains from the past is frequently under threat, and a general principle of malignant neglect of old buildings seems to prevail. Fortunately, in recent years some doughty battles have been fought here. Notable victories have been won by local people opposed to the cavalier attitude of developers and mindful of the losses of historical properties entailed in the construction of the pseudo-Swiss monstrosity. For those wishing to jeer at the stylistic excesses of the latter, take a look at the enormous, shield-shaped north-facing window visible from the top of Shire Hall Street. Anyone who wishes instead to celebrate the positive might seek out the sixteenth-century Vaynol Arms on Palace Street, rescued from demolition in 1995 and now restored, and the plainly elegant eighteenth-century houses at 6 and 8 High Street, which were snatched from the council's philistine jaws at the last moment by public enquiry in 1991. They will surely also be encouraged to note signs of resurgence and returning life: in the newly refurbished market hall of 1832, with its wrought-ironwork, bare wood, balcony cafe, music, flower and jewellery stalls; along Stryd Twll yn y Wal (Hole in the Wall Street), with its excellent bookshop and bistros; at Porth yr Aur (the Golden Gate), where a budget hostel and pavement cafe speak of the people reclaiming streets the planners had rendered moribund.

Maybe after all, though, the presiding images of Caernarfon are to be had on summer evenings when the sun slants low over the sandflats of Abermenai, the valerian in cracked walls dances in the breeze and beech copses across the straits stand evocatively against the light; or on a soft November night on the western esplanade beneath the walls, a ghostly local fishing boat back from the bay stealing between buoys into the harbour mouth, mist hushing over the ramparts, whispering tinted and stealthy around the street-lamps, carrying with it voice upon voice, accent upon accent, sound upon sound from the echoes of history. Time and again javelin and goose-quilled shaft have been loosed, wuthering, on to these sea-winds, and hang there now forever. This is a unique town.

Above it the hills swell southwards, the first group a triptych – Moel Smytho, Moel Tryfan and Mynydd Cilgwyn – pocked and strewn with quarries and their waste. These quarries were for the most part on a smaller scale than Dinorwig or Penrhyn, and had a less acrimonious history. Glynllifon, between the Porthmadog and Pwllheli roads out of Caernarfon, is the great estate of the Lords Newborough who made their money from them, and its present usage as tertiary college and school treat venue moderates my attitude towards it. The house is a poor early Victorian version of classical, but Fort Williamsburg, in the grounds a little to the south-east, is more intriguing in a child's-mentality way. It has tunnels, walls, moats, and lookouts, and it is crowned by a flimsy little tower. Most of it was built by the first Lord Newborough in the mid-eighteenth century so that he could play at soldiers here. It's all neglected now, weedy and overgrown. Children love it; they might properly, in their weakness and vulnerability, inhabit its fantasy world of slits and embrasures, castellations, magazines, gateways, and all the small-scale ostentation of power. Around it, the sheltering trees of the estate are particularly fine – giant firs soar thirty metres above the undergrowth that is invading and strangling the life out of the more delicate foreign species, planted here under the secular lord's protection and now struggling for their very survival among hardier and more vigorous common and native plants.

It's difficult to take seriously the idea that the good Lord Newborough drilled his militia here in this child's playground, that he used it as focus for the two societies he founded, 'The Garrison at Fort Williamsburg' and the 'Holy Order of Sisterhood United Connected and Regulated with the Free Firm and Friendly Garrison at Williamsburg'. I begin to suspect a joke. Was our dear old Lord a humorist? Was his estate dedicated to children's play? Was he less formidable than my imagination has so far assumed? When you begin to think along those lines, within the walls of Glynllifon – if you can forget for the moment their purpose to exclude – there's plenty of evidence to suggest that the architect of these grounds was more interested in the comic sublime than the cosmic sublime: a tiny boathouse, a children's water mill, grottoes, pretend cromlechs, ponds and caverns with roof-lights. Even on sombre afternoons they have a gleam of fun about them. I understand why children like to visit the place, to play in avenues lit by the autumn brilliance of maple and the translucent glow of beech leaves. And then you find a plaque:

> This tribute is dedicated by the Transport and General Workers' Union in Wales to the North Wales slate quarrymen, their families, novelists and poets who between them interwove the language, history and culture of this part of Wales. Through dignity in their work they gave of themselves so that others may understand.

I don't think the stiffness of language and echo of war's inflated rhetoric there is unintentional. On a little slope just beyond is a structure, a jumble of blocky concrete spelling out *Chwalfa* (dispersal) – a representation of a ruined cottage with its *aelwyd* (hearth) cold and empty, but with the message *'nid oes bradwr yn y tŷ hwn'* (no traitor, no blackleg, in this house). The sculpture's called *'Gwerin y Graith'* (People of the Scar), and I find it curiously ambiguous. Is the sculptor saying that those who stood out against the employers' oppressions in the quarry lock-outs brought their houses to ruin, let their hearths grow cold, sent fever and starvation into their children's schools? If so, this memorial should properly be sited in Penrhyn Castle's grounds; the Newborough family were more enlightened. When you look up from here, your eye travels beyond the wall's confines to the former commons of Cilgwyn and Fron, with their abandoned quarries and mountains of spoil. It was the first Lord Newborough who opposed Crown Leases and entrepreneurial exploitation of this land, and championed the cause and right of small, independent quarrymen to work its slate seams. How does that fact sit with the placing of this statement in concrete on his former lands? The fantasy landscape of Glynllifon, with its complexity of signs, induces in me a state of confusion and challenges my beliefs. And if that was part of the intention of the designer of these grounds, or of the more recent artists who have augmented his work, I congratulate them now or across the years for pointing up, to those of us who carry beliefs, the necessity always

IOLO WILLIAMS

Iolo Williams, Royal Society for the Protection of Birds Species Officer for Wales, sits opposite me in a Beddgelert cafe and lists what Wales has lost: 'We've got no industry any more, the destruction of habitat through forestry and farming has been dire, there's no longer a rugby team worth speaking of.' At the last he pulls a particularly long face, and you guess from the physical presence of the man that it's a subject dear to his heart – 'but at least we've made a success of the red kite, and its survival's a source of real national pride. You even get farmers in Mid-Wales who'll tell you how much it means to them.'

For the last several years Iolo's been a sort of

one-man ornithological army, protecting the birds of Wales from the depredations of shooters, game-keepers and egg-collectors – all the various enemies who covertly threaten the things he loves, the wild birds in which the country abounds. Of egg-collectors, he's vitriolic in his condemnation: 'If I were a dictator, I'd hang them,' he states, and a passion lights up his cool, grey eyes so that you don't doubt his sincerity. If I were an egg-collector ('a peculiar breed – stupid Victorian throwbacks'), I'd keep well out of the way of this man, even more so when he has the frequent voluntary assistance of the SAS or the Gurkhas to help him guard nests of rare birds in the breeding seasons: 'They regard it as good training – patient, covert surveillance operations. The thieves don't know what's hit them at times.'

He's first-language Welsh, born in Llanfair ym Muallt ('The doctor who delivered me was one of the wardens in Rhandirmwyn when the kites were at their lowest, and that's where my mother reckons I got the fascination with birds from'), the son of a headmaster who settled in Llanwddyn when Iolo was five and stayed in the job there for twenty-two years. Iolo remembers Welsh as language of the playground then and laments its passing in that area now: 'A lot of Maldwyn has attracted incomers, so inevitably the language has gone.' He went on to secondary school in Llanfyllin and hated it: 'I used to get off the school bus in the morning and miss assembly, just go out in the woods watching birds till it was time for the bus home. My mum would ask why I was all filthy, which was from climbing the trees, so I'd tell her I'd been fighting.'

Despite the loathing for school, he scraped enough A-levels to win a place on a pioneering ecology course at North East London Polytechnic, where he played rugby five days a week, emerged with a decent degree and then moved back to Wales. He took contract work with the RSPB and the late-lamented Nature Conservancy Council, an environmental watchdog whose teeth became so sharp that the government had it put down: 'They were the best working times I've had – no responsibilities, just go out and count birds.' Decision-time came for him seven years ago. He was offered an RSPB job on Speyside, golden eagles an incentive there, at the same time as one in Wales. He stayed. He already seems to know every inch of his home country, every fledgling reared in it. When he retires in thirty years' time, Iolo Williams will be an institution – to birds what Evan Roberts was to the mountain flowers. I imagine him out there then, in Cwm Pennant maybe or the wild moors of the Berwyn he's known since childhood, the ravens and choughs wheeling round him, buzzards and kites drifting shyly overhead, and the lapwings scattering their pealing cries like laughter.

for openness, and the willingness to make exceptions and to revise. And then again, my eye travels up to those commons above with their scattered communities and relict former industry, and to two memorials to a woman whose enduring testimony of experience constitutes one of the profound achievements of Welsh literature in this or any century.

'If Kate Roberts had written in English,' a professor of that discipline fluent in Welsh once told me, 'she would single-handedly have sustained women's literary studies courses and the Virago backlist for decades.' Her birth-home of Cae'r Gors is an apt ruin preserved alongside the council houses in Rhosgadfan. The memorial plaque to her at the *Golygfa Lôn Wen* among the gorse and heather on Braich Moel Smytho has been vandalized and scratched with graffiti, but still it reads: *'Bu'r olygfa hon yn gyfrwng i adnewyddu ysbryd llawer ac yn ysbrydoliaeth i weithiau Kate Roberts o Rosgadfan 1891-1985.'* (This view has refreshed the spirits of many and inspired the writings of Kate Roberts of Rhosgadfan.) Daughter of a quarryman-crofter, a radical journalist and founding member of Plaid Cymru, she is a short-story writer and novelist of intense gravity and resonance, with a sure ear for the inflections and nuances of speech and clear, unflinching insight into character. Her work is rooted in this marred landscape with its transcendent culture, exigent lives and repressive morality. When Saunders Lewis asked her from what source her writing came, she answered:

> From the society in which I was brought up, a poor society in an age of poverty; for that reason I was not tempted to write stories dealing with sex, or the mutual struggles between people of different characters, or with the spiritual struggles of souls – it was always a struggle against poverty. But notice that the characters haven't reached the bottom of that poverty, they are struggling against it, are afraid of it.

That statement might be from an entirely different social stratum, but there is an obvious similarity of acceptance between it and Jane Austen's metaphor of the small piece of ivory on which she inscribed her art. Kate

Roberts exercises similar liberty of imaginative perception, humour and intense sensory awareness within her small but unconstraining place of creativity. She is one of the keys to an understanding of the former life of these communities of the slate hills. Pennar Davies sums her up best when he writes that her 'enduring virtue... is a moral realism. Her main characters, who are always women – her men are usually pretty poor specimens – are pitted against adverse circumstances; and though there is no confirming optimism we are left, as in the best work of Hardy, with a sense of the worthwhileness of life in spite of it all.'

When you look out from her memorial and see how beauty transcends even the blight visited by centuries on the scene, you understand how that can be so, and you're reminded too of a line from one of her finest short stories, *'Y Condemniedig'* (The Condemned), in which she comments of her quarryman subject, a victim of illness and repression who at the last comes to appreciate the small, everyday acts of the wife whom he had never allowed himself to know, that *'Pan oedd ar fin colli peth, dechreuodd ei fwynhau'* (When he was on the point of losing a thing, he began to enjoy it). In its universality, that grave, typical and concise moral shouldn't be lost on those who look out from her viewpoint. She is one of the great writers in these islands this century, and far too little of her work has been translated into English.

Across the hill behind the viewpoint, a track through the gorse and heather leads over the moor and through the gap between Mynydd Mawr – the 'elephant mountain', so called for its shape when seen from the direction of Caernarfon – and Moel Tryfan, where it divides into a network of paths descending past oak woodland and slate tips to Nantlle. The large lake behind the terraces of the village is called Llyn Nantlle Uchaf (Higher

OVERLEAF *Snowdon from Llyn Nantlle* is the subject of two of the great eighteenth-century artist Richard Wilson's most famous paintings. But the present-day scene is no longer as he viewed it, the lower of the two lakes formerly here having been drained at the end of the last century.

Nantlle Lake), which raises the obvious question where the lower one might be. In the two versions of Richard Wilson's 1765 painting of 'Snowdon from Llyn Nantlle', lower and upper lakes are clearly visible. On the first edition of the Ordnance Survey map for this area, published in 1840, the lower lake is still marked, the road skirting its northern margin, but already the quarry of Penyrorsedd is following the good rock down towards it. As the nineteenth century wore on, the workings of the Dorothea quarry in the valley bottom spread, went deeper, and flooding became a problem. So the Afon Llyfni was diverted and channelled, and in 1899 the lake too, which had provided the foreground for two of the masterpieces of eighteenth-century art, was drained, its bed used for dumping slate waste.

The defunct Dorothea quarry is now itself a lake of awe-inspiring depth – 250 metres – a popular venue for divers and scene of some fatalities. Since the 1970s its waterside terraces and abandoned buildings have given temporary shelter to communities of travellers. The first to come called itself the 'Friendship Family', squatted in derelict cottages with Tilley lamps, gas stoves and polythene across the windows, and made a living by selling seasoned pitch-pine timber from the quarry sheds. The 'rave' culture which arrived later ran into conflict with local residents and was evicted amidst intense ill-feeling, in which the frustrations of a proud and tight-knit former industrial community against its usage as a reservoir of cheap housing and arena for inconsiderate behaviour were given vehement voice. The respectful co-existence established in Bethesda and elsewhere proved impossible to achieve.

My own memories of the village in the 1960s centre around characters like Dafydd Nantlle, tall and powerful with a shock of white hair and piercing blue eyes, cycling off before daybreak on his upright black bicycle with a long, single-barrelled shotgun slung over his back, and returning at noon with a couple of foxes and perhaps a rabbit or two slung from the crossbar, the latter to eat, the former for their pelts and the bounty on their brushes. He was reputed to have shot at least 250 foxes every year since his youth, which gives an idea of what the fox population of these hills might be. And there was the octogenarian Mrs Myfanwy Williams of Nantlle Terrace, garrulous and hospitable in her back kitchen, who would tell you what she'd learnt as a young married woman in the 1930s on Workers' Educational Association courses run by the poet Robert Williams Parry. People like these, as well as the village's openness to the west and its position on the edge of the central hill massif, have always given Dyffryn Nantlle a distinctive atmosphere.

Let us come back to the paintings by Richard Wilson, which hang in Liverpool's Walker Art Gallery and Nottingham's Castle Museum – the Liverpool version is more delicately lit and my own favourite. They are both exquisitely composed canvases, in which the natural contours of the hills are adjusted and accentuated to achieve harmony and balance. A group of rustics – a white-shawled woman and two men fishing – stand in the foreground, framed by a dome of light reflected in the still lake, which leads the eye up from this scene of Arcadian contentment to the peak of Snowdon, rather elegantly and benignly grand and firmly integrated by the composition into the whole. The scene is washed in hazy, russet, glowing light. It's easy to see how so idealized a picture of peasantry peacefully coexisting with nature at the lower margin of an orderly universe appealed to the buyer of the painting, William Vaughan of Corsygedol in Ardudwy, Celtic Revivalist and the wealthiest landowner in that area.

In a different medium entirely, Nantlle is associated with another great masterpiece of European art. This is the final story, *Math fab Mathonwy*, of the *Pedair Cainc y Mabinogi* ('Four Branches of the Mabinogi' – since Lady Charlotte Guest's editing of the translation by John Jones and Thomas Price of a group of stories from *Llyfr Coch Hergest*, the eleven stories from this manuscript have generally been known in translation as *The Mabinogion*; there are two current translations, that of Gwyn Jones and Thomas Jones, published by Dent, being much the superior). *Math fab Mathonwy* is a long and complex bundle of themes, embodying many folk-tale motifs, which are handled by its final anonymous redactor with remarkable skill and fluency.

DEWI JONES

I first met Dewi Jones from Penygroes when I was making a television series on the history of the Welsh mountains. We needed an expert on the early guides in Snowdonia and it was mentioned that there was a man in Dyffryn Nantlle who knew a great deal about them. So I went to see him and discovered an anachronism, a character in the direct tradition of the early botanical and recreational guides, someone who might have stepped, self-improved, straight from the pages of Victorian fiction. He's a rotund, intent character.

His looks and dark hair belie his fifty-four years. He lives in a neat house by the crossroads in the little quarry town. I arrived there in a shower of rain and he left me in the parlour, inspecting two cases of rare books about Wales, Ireland, botany and mountaineering as he went to make tea, which duly arrived strong and in cups of delicate porcelain. We sat down to talk.

Was I aware, he asked, that in this very house had lived William Morris Parry, who, with Gwallter Llyfni ('Sylvanus'), in 1930 had founded

Cymdeithas Hanesyddol Dyffryn Nantlle (Dyffryn Nantlle Historical Society)? Gwallter, he went on, was one of a great trio of friends who were collectors and enthusiasts for the natural and local history of their home region, the others being Bob Owen Croesor and Carneddog, who lived in the lovely farmhouse of Carneddi above Nantmor. Dewi's enthusiasm clearly stated all this as the tradition he is proud to uphold. And to add a human touch, he recounted how Sylvanus liked his pint, and that he and Carneddog, who was a teetotaller, would exchange teasing *englynion* (verses) on that topic. He added that poor Gwallter was consumptive; he died in 1932 at the age of forty-nine and is buried down the road in Llanllyfni churchyard.

To lighten the mood, he opened cupboards in his tidy parlour, showed me texts of lectures he delivers for the Workers' Educational Association each winter, and let me look through the meticulous card index he keeps of species of plant seen each year, with notes on habitat, variation and number. And then, since the rain had ceased, he suggested we venture out to record some more.

We drove round to Cwm Llefrith, and set off across sedgy moorland to an area of tufa bluffs, hung with vegetation and with a lively stream dashing through them. The place was a garden. Honeysuckle hung down, and rose-root, wild thyme and golden rod. But Dewi had lower interests. Stooping by the stream he peered under boulders and into crevices masked by a shimmer of spray, made little delighted noises of pleasure and identification and introduced me to the species he had found: Hard Shield Fern (his main interest is pteridology, the study of ferns), Hay-scented Buckler Fern ('if you rub the spores the scent's that of new-mown hay'), Holly Fern, Broad Buckler Fern. He scurried over the rocks with remarkable agility, scanning around every so often to locate remembered natural markers which lead him to the plants he seeks.

'It was in a valley near here that John Lloyd Williams, when a young schoolmaster in Garn Dolbenmaen, found the Killarney Fern, which is one of the rarest British plants. But after he'd announced his discovery, he was followed to the site and it was stripped, which was the common fate for most ferns at the hands of the collectors in Victorian times.'

'So the Killarney Fern's entirely gone now?' I asked. He gave me an enigmatic look: 'Would you like to see it?' A bargain was struck. No details of its precise location were to be disclosed. We walked back to the car, drove a mile or two and walked a mile or two more to a plain, undistinguished hillside with a scatter of nondescript outcrops across it. Above one of them an oozing patch of sphagnum dripped constantly into a narrow cleft. Dewi beckoned me down, regardless of the water pouring on us. Across the floor of the cleft was a small, dull-green, low plant, on Dewi's face an expression of pure exultation.

Even if I had Dewi's permission to do so, I could never take you or find my way back to the place where the Killarney Fern grows. There are some things which go beyond attentiveness to the alchemy of instinctive knowledge. Simples-collectors is how these men and women used to be known, each one of them what in Welsh would be called *'dyn ei filltir sgwâr'* (a man of his own square mile). Their simplicity lives on in Dewi, so perpetuating its own fine portion of genius.

The hero of the narrative is Lleu Llaw Gyffes (Fair and Deft-handed), from whose name Nantlle is commonly supposed to derive – the valley's junior school is called *Ysgol Bro Lleu* (School of the Region of Lleu). When Lleu is miraculously born of Math's niece Aranrhod in the course of a maidenhood test devised by the magician Math, he is snatched up and nurtured by the enchanter Gwydion. But when he meets his mother she places upon him a triple curse, each stage of which is added as the previous one is fulfilled: he shall have no name unless she herself gives it to him, never wear arms unless she herself bestows them, and 'never have a wife of the race that is now on this earth'. This part of the story is grounded in the features and place-names in the vicinity of Dyffryn Nantlle, as is a further episode, when Gwydion, guided by a sow, finds Lleu in the form of a wounded eagle in a tree-top in Nantlle – but we'll come to that in the next chapter. The degree to which the narrative chimes with the region's names imparts to the traveller here something of the enchantment of the tale itself.

Nantlle has one other masterpiece of an entirely different kind. It's a piece of fine carving, very much of its own place. It used to stand half a mile above the village on a terrace of the abandoned Penyrorsedd quarry – a fitting, desolate shrine, looking out to Drwsycoed, the peerless ridge opposite, and Snowdon. Perhaps it was feared that up there it would be vandalized, for now, more prosaically, it shelters discreet and unknown in the garden of the *Eglwys Bresbyteraidd Cymru Baladeulyn* (Baladeulyn Welsh Presbyterian Church). Half obscured by leaves, it's a Great War memorial.

What makes this slab of slate, with its minimal text – *'Er gof am…A Gwympasant'* (In memory of…who fell) – and eighteen names, something entirely out of the ordinary is the frieze that surrounds the roll of honour. Incised with painstaking delicacy and strength of vision into the single slab are four scenes: quarry rock-men in a pit with a Blondin (a carrying-cradle running on wire cables) above them; work in a cutting shed; an incline and wagons (on one of which, quite reverently, some wag has added a CND sign); and finally, across the bottom, a war scene of dead trees, ruins, hunched soldiers and huge guns. The images revolve, echo, run into each other disturbingly; the design is stark, naive, lived-through. In the tautness of line, the scenes have something of the quality of those marvellous drawings by Henri Gaudier-Brzeska in Manchester Art Gallery. No one seems to know whose work it is. I know of nothing else quite like it. Its craftsmanship and clear record speak volumes about the culture which produced it.

There are two ways we could continue from Nantlle. If we walked the way the eye is led in Richard Wilson's scene, we'd pass by the old copper mines of Drwsycoed, which are rumoured, without historical evidence, to date back to the thirteenth century and to have been visited by Edward I. It's curious that the Romans, indefatigable metallurgists that they were, should not have discovered these surface-outcropping lodes, for their roads passed both top and bottom of the valley. But it was left for Victorian prospectors to exploit the mineral riches. The slopes to the south of the road in particular are honeycombed with their workings, the deepest of which are the deepest in Snowdonia, their shafts going down 200 metres. Still accessible, they are deadly dangerous. These were once some of the most profitable mines in Britain – it's estimated that in the region of 30,000 tons of high-grade copper ore were extracted from them – though by the time of their final closure in 1931 their best years were long past. 'Landscaping' has taken place at Drwsycoed in recent years, and the waste and mine-buildings that used to crowd the valley floor in the shadow of Craig y Bere's bizarre and crumbling ridges have been effectively concealed.

Another set of disappearing acts locates at the top of the pass, where the ragged-margined and rocky Llyn y Dywarchen (Lake of the Turf) is to be found. Giraldus, in the twelfth century, records that it had 'a wandering island, which strays mostly with the force of the wind impelling it to

OVERLEAF Travellers on the road which passes within a few metres could easily miss Llyn y Dywarchen (Lake of the Turf), which would be a pity, for this lake has associated with it a wealth of local tradition concerning the fairies, who were once supposed to live hereabouts in great numbers.

opposite sides of the lake. Sometimes cattle grazing on it are, to the surprise of shepherds, suddenly carried across to more distant parts.' Edmund Halley, the astronomer, verified on a visit in 1698 that the island was present and did indeed float, but raising of water level by damming in the mid-nineteenth century finally dispatched the phenomenon, which according to Giraldus was little more than pieces of the peaty bank breaking off from time to time.

When the island did float, its most interesting occupant was a fairy. The story goes that a young man from Drwsycoed farm was in the habit of watching the fairies, present in this area in great number; this is good fairy country, its rushy cwms, smooth hills, river-banks and lake-borders hiding the entrances to their lands. One night, on the bank of Llyn y Dywarchen, he saw a fairy of particular beauty and abducted her, keeping her under iron lock and key in his house while endeavouring to win her affections. She refused to marry him, but consented to be his servant if he could find out her name. By chance, returning from market one night, he eavesdropped on a fairy conversation and discovered it. So she became his servant, and as he slowly won her confidence, so too, on condition that he never touched her with iron, did she agree to marry him. But if the condition was broken she was free to return to her own family. They had children – a boy and a girl – and lived happily for some years. But the inevitable happened: he touched her by accident with a bridle and she vanished instantly. Thereafter, in one version of the legend, she visits him once only, singing a verse through his window on a frosty night:

> *Rhag bod annwyd ar fy mab,*
> *Yn rhodd rhowch arno gob ei dad.*
> *Rhag bod annwyd ar liw'r can*
> *Yn rhodd rhowch arni bais ei mam.*

(Lest it be cold for my son/Put on him his father's smock./Lest it be cold with the fair one/Put on her her mother's petticoat.) In another version, with her mother's help, the fairy-wife Bela is enabled to meet her husband on the floating island for as long as he lives. Much the same story is told about Braich y Ddinas, over the hill in Cwm Pennant, and T. Gwynn Jones, in his seminal study of Welsh folklore, comments that in Eifionydd the inhabitants of Cwm Pennant were called *Belisiaid* because of their supposed descent from the fairies. The explanation by W. J. Gruffydd of the fairy/lake associations throughout Wales has long had currency: 'It is probable that, when the iron-using Celtic invaders became the dominant race, the previous inhabitants, perhaps for a very long time, lived a separate and secluded life of their own in some kind of lake-dwelling or in isolated and inaccessible parts.'

All this material must have constituted some part of the hearth-talk at the school-house of Rhyd Ddu, just down from the pass on the summit of which Llyn y Dywarchen glints, in the last decade of the last century for a boy who was to become an outstanding literary figure in Wales. The school-house is now an outdoor pursuits centre for the children of Gwynedd. For its most famous former inhabitant, '*yr oedd popeth yno – tad a mam, brawd a chwaer, mab a merch, heb sôn am fwyd a diod, tân a chysgod, llyn ac afon, mynydd a nefoedd*' (everything was there – father and mother, brother and sister, boy and girl, let alone food and drink, fire and shelter, lake and stream, mountain and sky). As poet, essayist and literary critic, Sir T. H. Parry-Williams, born here in 1887, is, with Saunders Lewis and Kate Roberts, one of the three pre-eminent Welsh literary figures of this century. The first *modern* Welsh poet, he came to prominence through the unprecedented feat of winning both Crown and Chair in the *Eisteddfod Genedlaethol* (National Eisteddfod) at Wrexham in 1912, and again at Bangor in 1915 – a feat not repeated until the successes of Alan Llwyd in 1973 and 1976.

Parry-Williams's controversial poem on the given subject of *Y Ddinas* (The City), which won the Crown in 1915, marked a shift away from late nineteenth-century poeticizing and early twentieth-century romanticizing. It was the only one of his four prize entries to be published, and then only in a small private edition as late as 1962. Moralistic in almost an eighteenth-century style – Dr Johnson's Juvenalian satire '*London*' is not too distant a

Still inscribed with its maker's name, Dingey & Sons, Truro, this fine
waterwheel was carried up into Cwm Ciprwth in sections on the
backs of ponies over a hundred years ago and installed to drain a
copper mine. Recently restored by the National Park Authority,
it stands solitary and intact high above Cwm Pennant.

relative – it ponders a labourer reflecting on suicide and then committing it; a hedonistic young girl who ends up as a prostitute; an artist tortured by the unattainable images of his vision; and a wealthy woman whose life, if anything, is the emptiest of all. It raised a storm of protest. One adjudicator, the minor lyricist Eifion Wyn, dissociated himself from the award, saying that the poem's 'content is immodest, its teaching unsafe, and its tone ignoble'. More informally, he snarled that it was a poem about 'suicides and whores'. It stands in much the same relationship to twentieth-century Welsh poetry as *The Waste Land* does to poetry in English. It, and the freedoms it gained, were vastly influential, and gave a foretaste of the mature work of Parry-Williams, where plain, colloquial diction engages strikingly with the complexity of a world whose savagery and contradictions confuse the poet, and in which his anchors – however they may drag – are the tangible realities of his birthplace:

> *Ac yno mae'r clogwyni, a'r niwl yn niwl,*
> *A Medi'n Fedi o hyd, ac un ac un yn ddau.*

(And there are the cliffs, and the mist is mist,/And September's still September and one and one make two.)

Perhaps you come closest to the essential Parry-Williams in the rootedness and near-mystical relationship to landscape expressed in poems like 'Oerddwr' – the name's that of a farm, unvisited and aloof, on the shaggy hillside above Pont Aberglaslyn:

> *Nid daear mo'r ddaear yno, nid haen o bridd;*
> *Mae ansylweddoldeb dan donnen pob cae a ffridd...*
> *O feudy'r Cwm hyd at feudy'r Hendre draw*
> *Y mae llwybrau'n arwain i leoedd a fu neu ddaw.*

(Earth is not earth there, no mere crust of soil;/There is insubstantiality under each calloused field and sheepwalk.../From the cowshed at Cwm to Hendre beyond/Paths lead to places past or unborn.)

As if to illustrate Parry-Williams's point, the farm of Clogwyn y Gwin, just above Rhyd Ddu, has a macabre connection with the last shot to be fired at the Battle of Waterloo. After the battle was over, runs the tale, a son of Clogwyn y Gwin was lying wounded among the dead and dying with a bullet in his knee-cap when he saw an old woman moving about nearby, robbing the corpses of their valuables and despatching those who still breathed and groaned with a hammer she carried. She saw him raise his head and nodded to him as though to say 'I'll deal with you presently', so he lifted himself up on an elbow, took careful aim with his musket, let off a round and she went head over heels dead – 'and that was the last shot to be fired at Waterloo'.

From Rhyd Ddu the moorland valley of Nant Colwyn drops down to Beddgelert, its western flanks inked out by conifers. Above them is the cliff in which modern tradition places Ogof Owain Glyndŵr, the cave in which the Welsh leader is reputed to have hidden after the failure of his uprising, succoured and provisioned by the Prior of Beddgelert. The quality of accommodation – a dank ledge covered in nettles beneath dripping over-hangs – is hardly of heroic status. If you wish to reach it, follow a slippery ledge running out from the gully on the left facing the cliff and take care, for there's a 90-metre drop below the narrowest section. Having found the cave, you might be disappointed to learn that the Reverend David Jenkins, in *Beddgelert: its Facts, Fairies, and Folklore* – a classic and rare work of local history published in 1899 – comprehensively rubbishes this association and tells us that the cave is in fact 'the opening in the dent of the rock' (i.e. the gully to the right), and that its name is Ogof Elen.

The forestry-drowned cwm beneath has a remarkable story attached. Its farm, Meillionen, was held in the late eighteenth century by two lonely old bachelors who originated from Lleyn. One winter's night a stranger arrived in their kitchen, and told them of a matter that troubled him. He was from Anglesey, and had dreamt of a pitcherful of money buried under a stone in a ruin called Hafod Ernallt on Meillionen land. In a manner entirely credible to those who know Welsh farmers, the old men, having heard the story, threw him off the scent by telling him that he must mean Meillionydd, a farm in Penllyn a day or more's walk away. Next morning, when the stranger had gone, the brothers went straight to the ruin, found the stone where he'd foretold, and under it sixty pounds' weight of gold and silver and a rare old shield, which was shown to Thomas Pennant during his tour through Wales in 1784. The brothers, it's recorded, became suddenly rich and one of them married. The duped stranger fades from the story.

Which is as good a way as any of introducing Beddgelert. On most days of the year visitors crowd into its narrow, pretty confines, admire its best-kept village awards and mill about in search of things to buy. Most of them end up visiting the supposed site of the grave of Gelert-the-faithful-hound (the village's name means Celert's grave). If they'll buy that they'll buy anything. It was erected by Mr David Prichard of the Royal Goat Hotel some time after his establishment had been built in 1801, as a means of increasing its trade. If the hoteliers of the village had any conscience or sense of gratitude, his statue would adorn the bridge. With that thought, let's return to Nantlle and take from there the opposite direction of travel.

A back road from the end of Nantlle Terrace leads through the old Dorothea workings to the quarry village of Talysarn, former home of two more of the astonishing array of talented people from this small area. There is an interesting tension between these two. The first is John Jones, Calvinistic Methodist preacher, whose self-denying ordinances thundered out, thrice every Sunday when not engaged elsewhere, from the pulpit of Capel Mawr between 1828 and his death in 1857. (We visited his Dolwyddelan birthplace in Chapter One.) The second is another great modern Welsh poet, who,

OVERLEAF 'Oh Lord, why did you make Cwm Pennant so beautiful/And an old shepherd's life so short?' wrote the poet Eifion Wyn. It's hard not to feel sympathy for the sentiment when you look on the effortless, swooping ridges which gather round the head of this loveliest of Welsh valleys.

despite the small total of his poetic output – it runs only to two slim volumes – touches peculiarly and unforgettably on the emotions of his readers. There is a blocky little memorial to him at the village crossroads which reads 'Robert Williams Parry 1884-1956'. He was cousin to Parry-Williams, and like him an Eisteddfod winner, taking the Chair at Colwyn Bay in 1910 with his *awdl* (poem in strict metres), *'Yr Haf'* ('The Summer'). Yet the two are quite different – the one a questing metaphysician, the other a quietly observant celebrant of nature and occasional critic of humanity whose closest kinship in English (or Anglo-Welsh!) poetry might be with Edward Thomas. The following sonnet, cast in the form of question and response between a resident and a visitor who's heard the *Mabinogi* story, is a strange, equivocal, balanced poem, whose questioning and pointed resignation is typically Welsh:

Does ond un llyn ym Maladeulyn mwy:
A beth a ddaeth o'r ddâr ar y ddol?

Daeth dau wareiddiad newydd i'n dau blwy:
Ac ni ddaw Lleu i Ddyffryn Nantlleu'n ol.

Pwy'r rhain sy'n disgyn hyd ysgolion cul
Dros erchyll drothwy chwarel Dorothea?

Y maent yr un mor selog ar y Sul
Yn Saron, Nasareth a Cesarea.

A glywsant hanes Math yn diwyd weu
Deunydd breuddwydion yn y bröydd hyn?
A glywsant hanes Gwydion yntau'n creu
Dyn o aderyn yma rhwng dau lyn?

Clywsant am ferch a wnaeth o flodau'r banadl
Heb fawr gydwybod ganddi, dim ond anadl.

(Only one lake now in the valley of two,/ And what's become of the oak-tree was in the meadow?/ *Two new civilizations have come to our two parishes:/ And Lleu will not return to Dyffryn Nantlle./* Who are these, descending narrow ladders/ Over the dreadful brink of Dorothea Quarry?/ *They are as ardent on Sunday/ In Saron, Nasareth and Cesarea./* Have they heard of Math's carefully weaving/ The web of dreams in these parts?/ And heard the story of Gwydion's creating/ Man from bird here between the lakes?/ *They've heard of a woman he made from flowers of the broom,/ Without much conscience in her, only breath.*)

What's crucial in this sonnet is the abrupt, dismissive tone of the responses, and the citing of the significant word *cydwybod* – conscience – the target at which John Jones's strictures were unerringly aimed from Capel Mawr pulpit, in the hard light of which the magical reduced at best to the merely moral, more often to the dubious and immoral. The opposition between poet's sympathies and pulpit strictures is made even more plain as we climb to the watershed of the ridge that bounds Dyffryn Nantlle to the south. I used to see this ridge against the sunset every night from the valley below during the years I lived there, and biased though I may be, it is for me the most sublime natural form I've ever looked on. When I see it at a distance from the hills away to the south it raises my spirits. I find it difficult to describe except by analogy with music. It has the plangency and melodious strength of a Beethoven late quartet or of Schubert's finest *Lieder*. The ridge-walk along it is one of the most memorable in Britain, the cwms which lie beneath – Cwm Silyn especially – as architectonic as any in Wales. And beneath it is Cwm Pennant.

There is a famous, and it has to be said rather sentimental, poem written at about the turn of the century by Eifion Wyn, which has the name of this valley as its title. Most Welsh speakers can recite at least a couple of lines from it, their voices often as not tinged with irony: '*Pam, Arglwydd, y gwnaethost Gwm Pennant mor dlws/ A bywyd hen fugail mor fyr?*' (Why, Lord, did you make Cwm Pennant so lovely/ And an old shepherd's life so short?)

ABOVE The slate mill at Ynysypandy, Cwm Ystradllyn, is cathedral-like in its grandeur. Unfortunately, its architectural excellence implied no measure of economic good sense. The quarry it was built to service provided little workable rock, and the grandiose scheme of which it was a part foundered within ten years.

RIGHT The dramatic coastline running north from Nefyn to Trefor was, until earlier this century, important for its granite-quarrying industry. Nowadays the old quarrying village of Porth y Nant has been taken over and restored by enthusiasts who exploit a rich seam of interest in the revival of the Welsh language.

The thought is commonplace enough, though no less affecting for that. What's more interesting is the unease which that customary, distanced delivery suggests. For explanation, we are back beneath the pulpit of Capel Mawr, the strictures reverberating – against, against, against! Beauty is an outlaw, a moral renegade that seeks to entrap and ensnare in earthly life the paradise-seeking soul. Renunciation, submission, plainness, labour! Not for these pew-bound generations the acts of attention which are the profoundest prayer, but acquiescence in a short, brutal life to secure happy exodus for the soul. Religion and the rise of capitalism is written into the ambivalent love the Welsh have for their land (it might be noted here that John Jones was for several years manager of the Dorothea quarry). The all-licensed poet can celebrate beauty and desire the future years, but his message was for too long shouted down as dangerous illusion from the pulpit for us to be at ease with it yet. And yet our instincts still reach back to an older time, prelapsarian, magically unreal except at the times we are confronted by it. We are back with the Williams Parry of his most famous sonnet, which records an after-chapel fleeting encounter with a fox up here on this sublime ridge a hundred metres from the hill summit. Williams Parry sees the fox as I see him now, as I have seen him so often, caught in poised surprise with one paw hesitantly held up, keen muzzled and the fires of his eyes upon me: *'Llwybrei-ddiodd ei ryfeddod prin o'n blaen'* (The rare wonder of it appeared before us).

This, the sonnet itself, is the watershed. It looks anew not on the return on investment in God, the message which thundered out from the pulpit below, but on – if you like to phrase it thus – the work of God which is nature. *'Ei ryfeddod prin'*: the rare wonder of it! Through the years I lived in Cwm Pennant that sense of wonder grew on me: that here was a landscape where every field-corner was thick with ghosts, where generations had played some cosmic chess-game, arranged and re-arranged stones into the temporary shapes of two or three hundred years, borrowed from here to build there, let frost and wind collapse and the grass wipe clean. *'Y mae lleisiau a drychiolaethau ar hyd y lle'*, wrote Parry-Williams – 'There are voices and phantoms throughout the place'. It is one of the half-dozen valleys which can claim to be loveliest in this most lovely of all countries: streams and woods, close turf with orchids and scabious, church and chapel, ridge and dome of hill, rough scree and a drift of bluebells like wood-smoke across a green shade, all intermingled, all shaken up together in this valley-vessel with its cliffed spur of Craig Isallt stopping up the end. The peregrines in Cwm Trwsgl — I've seen so often the tiercel attract the falcon from her nest, she flying under him and upside down to catch the pigeon he dropped to her, then breaking away and back to the inaccessible ledge as he sported about her. And yes, the foxes, which are supposed to be so alert — yet one passed me among the summit rocks of Moel Hebog one morning, coat glistening rich chestnut in the just-risen sun, my dog and I sitting quite still and he not three metres away so that his acrid stink had my bitch quivering in excitement. Other evenings in the summer, the cubs played outside their earth in a bank by Brithdir, delicately marked, robustly quarrelsome. And lest you think me oversentimental, one dark dog-fox ran through my flock of geese in clear mid-morning, tearing off a wing here, a shrieking head there, as I watched helplessly from the hillside above.

Not that foxes are the only killers. There were summer nights on the river when the foxglove bloomed and Owen John Cwt-y-Bugail and I patrolled our favourite water, where I held the lamp and carried the heavy battery as he poised, *trifar* in hand, fiercely intent, eyes glittering-cold as any soldier's hewing limbs at Pilleth or Mortimer's Cross 500 years before; then the shaft's plunge into dark pool, thrash and gleam of the stricken fish. Once the bailiff came along; there were two women with us that night and no chance of escape. Two of us hid behind a bush, fish and lamp among the roots of a tree. Owen John and his friend were on the grass, she pulling him down on top of her when the bailiff flashed his lamp: 'Oh, sorry mate, have one for me while you're at it!' And away he went.

The people were as much a part of the spirit of the place as river or hills: old faces, lingering conversations, the companionable crises of the farmer's

Out of the patchwork landscape of the Lleyn Peninsula rise sudden hills. Garn Fadryn, an extinct volcano, is one of them, and as with all the others, scattered across its top is extensive evidence of its occupation in prehistoric times - the walls and huts of which are now almost submerged in the heather.

year – the frenetic sweat and itch of stacking hay in a barn, pandemonious sadism at the sheep-dipping, the shepherding; that time in the late snow, the sheep tired with long labour and no option but to bare your arm to the elbow, push the breech lamb up and round before pulling it out, the lamb and your arm both marbled bloody and yellow against the white ground, and a few days later, in a field which the warming sun had now patched with green, a hare reared up to box with this same lamb. I remember all this. I remember from the early 1970s the young man from the gentle 'hippy' colony at Tanygraig who, desiring to live off the land's bounty, gathered the roots of a riverside plant and grated them into his salad. It was hemlock water dropwort. Within an hour he died in agony. The Vicar of Beddgelert, Martin Riley, despite disapproval, blessed and buried his ashes in the church-yard of Llanfihangel y Pennant, where they still lie, on the left as you enter the gate, under a painted slate.

I remember talking with old Mr Morus of Gilfach, asking him why sheep's heads hung in the trees above the stream by his house:

'*Duw*, it's cure for the *pendro*. When the sheeps die, I cut off its head and hang it there. Blowfly lays eggs, maggots eat the brain, fall into the stream, and the sickness is washed from the land.'

You will not find beliefs like that current if you go to Cwm Pennant these days. It has changed. A stiff knot of baling twine secures the rusting chapel-gate. Acre-millionaires and seekers of subsidies have bought into the valley. My old friends no longer farm their land, now fenced around with wire. The huge grey wintering sheds of corrugated iron dominate. It is made to work to repay investment in it. Rather than this exploitation, I am not sure that I do not prefer the old unease at its beauty, which spoke at least of the mystery of the place, and of a certain reverence. You can no longer buy tea from the fairies' descendants at Braich y Ddinas, for public health regula-tions have deemed its facilities sub-standard – a fate meted out to most of the best cafes I have known over the last forty years. Nor can you watch the badgers on moonlit nights as you sit on the plinth below the folly tower built in 1821 by Sir Joseph Huddart to commemorate his knighthood, the beech trunks glimmering and the animals' coats glistening and bouncing in their sociable frolics, for the tower's restored and private now, a holiday home. But you can at least still walk the old green mine-and-quarry tramway of 1875 from Blaen Pennant – the best and longest belvedere in Wales – which contours round high above the enchanted valley into its harsher eastern neighbour, Cwm Ystradllyn.

Most visitors, on entering Cwm Ystradllyn, are struck by the grandeur of its cathedral. It deserves to be thought of like that, having been part of one of the most socially advanced projects in the history of North Walian industry – Gwynedd's counterpart to New Lanark. In fact, though, the building is Ynysypandy slate mill, the most elegant and impressive of Welsh industrial monuments, built between 1855 and 1857 as part of the Gorseddau quarry complex. A tramway was constructed down to Porthmadog, together with a village of thirty-six houses, Treforys, whose remains and street plan can be seen on the southern slopes of Moel Hebog above Plas-llyn. In 1861, forty-five people lived here. Ten years later it was deserted. The reason for the failure of a scheme that cost £50,000 – an enormous sum in those times – is not hard to discern. Look at the extent of the waste-spills alongside the mill, which had been equipped with the best and most modern machinery; they are tiny. The *Carnarvon & Denbigh Herald*, reporting the company's liquidation in 1871, noted that 'everything that could facilitate the works was produced, nothing being wanting but the slate vein.' If you walk to the quarry itself along the old tramway – at one point it runs beneath a standing wave of wall, curved over the track to protect it from stone-fall – nothing is more obvious than that this is not workable rock. It gives an intriguingly corrective slant to the notion of inexorable Victorian self-confidence.

From Cwm Ystradllyn, it's an easy matter to gain the shoulder of Moel Hebog called Braich y Gornel, where another abandoned settlement – this time dating from the Iron Age – is spread out before you, its huts, field-systems and burnt mounds scattered acrosss the hillside. The views from here are magnificent and improve all the while as you mount the final steepening slopes to the summit of Moel Hebog. This hill has as fine a prospect as any in Wales, the more so since the outlook encompasses the peninsula of Lleyn narrowing down, a sea at either hand, to Ynys Enlli: 'Either because of its pure air, which comes across the sea from Ireland, or through some miracle occasioned by the merits of holy men who lived there, this island has the peculiarity that no one dies there except in extreme old age, for disease is almost unheard of. In fact, no one dies there at all unless he is very old indeed. The bodies of a vast number of holy men are buried there', commented Giraldus, wistfully.

The island still feels like that now, out there at the end of the peninsula, remote and desirable with its seaward garden behind the sheltering hill. In the Middle Ages, three pilgrimages here were the equivalent of one to Rome, and *teithiau pererin* (pilgrims' ways) link old churches and holy wells on either side of the peninsula. The southern route skirts Porth Neigwl — Hell's Mouth is its English name — into which bay the poet R. S. Thomas looked from the windows of his cottage by Plas yn Rhiw through a quarter-century of the testing of his faith. The paths converge at Aberdaron, which is the seaside resort of childhood dream, and continue out to Ffynnon Fair, the holiest and least accessible well in Wales — salt-fretted, natural-shrined, lined with viridian weed, and figuring forth the Trinity in its shape.

There are other sites of resonance too: the prehistoric hilltop villages of Madryn, Boduan, Yr Eifl. And ones of more modern significance: the Welsh language centre housed in the old quarrying hamlet of Porth y Nant, which has its own strange triple-curse story, concerning Vortigern, from whom the valley takes its name of Nant Gwrtheyrn. He had a spat with the monks of Bangor; they prophesied that no one would marry in his settlement, none

OVERLEAF The bulky shape of Moel Hebog (hill of the hawk) blocks the end of Nant Gwynant. Farthest west of the great peaks of central Snowdonia, it is also one of the finest viewpoints in the area, looking widely out over Caernarfon and Cardigan Bays.

would be buried there and that the village would have no future. The story leaps to the last century: a young couple in the quarry village decide to defy the curse and marry in its chapel. After the ceremony, according to custom, the bride runs from the house for the husband to catch and carry back over the threshold. She is skittish, mischievous, and she disappears. He searches, the village searches, but she is not found. Years later, as an old man, he is wandering towards the grass-topped cliffs above the shore when a squall rolls in from the bay, lightning flickering before it. He shelters under a tree, which is struck by a shaft from the storm, the trunk splits and a skeletal arm swings out, bearing on its wedding finger a ring's gold gleam. Or so they'll tell you in the Llithfaen pub, Porth y Nant too being a place apart.

Perhaps the holiest story from Lleyn concerns one of the great acts of political protest this century – the burning, on 8 September 1936, of sheds at the RAF bombing range near Pwllheli, whose construction had, in Saunders Lewis's words, entailed the demolition of 'one of the most historic [houses] in Lleyn...a resting place for the Welsh Pilgrims to...Ynys Enlli...a thing of hallowed and secular majesty. It was taken down and utterly destroyed a week before we burnt on its fields the timbers of the vandals who destroyed it.' This action was undertaken by Saunders Lewis, the only peer of Kate Roberts and Sir T. H. Parry-Williams in the literary life of Wales this century; the Carmarthenshire prose-writer D. J. Williams, himself a beloved Welsh institution; and a Baptist minister, the Reverend Lewis Valentine. Saunders Lewis wrote: '...nothing could have been easier than for us to ask some of the generous and spirited young men of the Welsh Nationalist Party to set fire to the aerodrome and get away undiscovered. It would be the beginning of methods of sabotage and guerrilla turmoil. [We] determined to prevent any such development.'

The Welsh nation had been unanimous in its opposition to the bombing range's being located here. The alternative English sites had been breeding grounds for Dorset swans and Northumberland ducks, against which the interests and traditions of the cultural community of Wales were set at naught. Lewis, Williams and Valentine were tried in Caernarfon and, despite a biased summing up by the judge, the jury failed to agree a verdict. The trial shifted to the Old Bailey where the outcome was inevitable. Lewis again: 'If you find us guilty, you proclaim that the will of the Government may not be challenged by any person whatsoever, and that there is no appeal possible to morality...'

The three defendants were each sentenced to nine months in Wormwood Scrubs. Despite the shadow of war, they were on their release quietly feted by their own nation. Lewis alone was dismissed from his post as university lecturer in Welsh at Swansea – a shabby action which galvanized Williams Parry into the finest phase of his poetry. Then as now, it is a mistake ever to underestimate the attachment of Welsh people to their country and community, tradition and justice. With that thought, Lleyn for all its fascination being outside the remit of this book, we can slip quietly down from the summit of Moel Hebog, over Bryn Banog, past the spot where, in the eighteenth century, travellers recorded seeing the uprights – now no doubt in use as gateposts or incorporated into field walls – of a huge stone circle, and by neglected brackeny paths across the insubstantial earth of Oerddwr to Pont Aberglaslyn, whence we cross into a different landscape.

CHAPTER FOUR

EMPTY QUARTER

Visitors to Beddgelert – dog-lovers all, it's safe to suppose – should know that its former inhabitants thought less well of their canine companions than we do. Pont Aberglaslyn, by which we cross into the great empty quarter of Snowdonia, has a considerable folklore in which dogs play a crucial role. The bridge's construction is ascribed to the devil, whose part of the bargain is that he shall possess the soul of the first creature to cross it. In the most typical of these stories, Robin Ddu, a magician, is drinking in the nearby public house when the devil comes to tell him the work is complete. Robin agrees to inspect it, promises that his labours won't go unrewarded, and with scraps from a loaf he is carrying under his arm lures a little dog from the pub to follow him. When they arrive at the bridge Robin looks askance, and asks whether it will bear the weight of his loaf. The devil, boastful, tells him to throw it on and see. So Robin rolls the loaf across and the dog darts after it, thus fulfilling the bargain with the devil; with a roar of laughter, Robin goes back to his drinking companions.

I can't vouch for the truth of this story, but some of the detail is certainly correct. The pub was called Tafarn Telyn and bore a harp as its sign; it stood in the fishing village of twelve or fifteen houses and a quay whose remains are faintly discernible on the southern bank of the Glaslyn by the first tributary down from the bridge. This and Borth y Gest were *the* ports of Traeth

Dwyryd estuary – ever-changing patterns of water, sand and light.

Mawr – the estuary of the Afon Glaslyn – places of considerable trade right down to about 1780. Thereafter, Aberglaslyn went into decline, and construction of the embankment between Porthmadog and Boston Lodge – finished in 1811 – ensured its demise as a port. As a village, it was brutally killed off by the Enclosure Acts. In 1899, the Reverend David Jenkins wrote of the inhabitants of Aberglaslyn that 'they lived in a freehold plot of God's earth; not one of them had ever known what it was to pay rent for the cots of their village. In their innocence, they spoke of their estate as being in Chancery. But spying eagles found the carrion, and the question was how could they pounce on it..?'

Jenkins records how 'a certain Captain Wardle' did just that. On his instructions,

> three men and a bailiff drove up to the village and told the occupants…that they must quit at once, that their houses were to be unroofed. The helpless women began to weep and pleaded for some explanation. The only explanation they got was to see their furniture hurled out through the door. One poor fellow, Cadwaladr Roberts, was lying ill in bed; he was dragged down the ladder which connected the ground floor and his tiny bedroom, and left in the hands of the houseless neighbours until he found shelter in the Union of Penrhyndeudraeth [like several other Welsh workhouses, this later became a hospital, Minffordd in this case]. After this piece of daylight robbery, the property passed into the hands of David Williams, Esq., for some time M.P. for Merionethshire.

Memory of a more palatable immorality haunts Nantmor, the valley a mile or so east of Aberglaslyn. It was home in the fifteenth century to a clutch of poets, most eminent among whom was Dafydd Nanmor. His name is still commemorated in the name of the house of Cae Dafydd, but the poet himself had to flee into exile in South Wales in 1453 on account of verses written to Gwen o'r Ddôl, a married woman. In one poem, with brazen disregard for his own safety, he mocks her husband and with a blithe unconcern for gender compares her to a peacock. His departure thereafter seems to

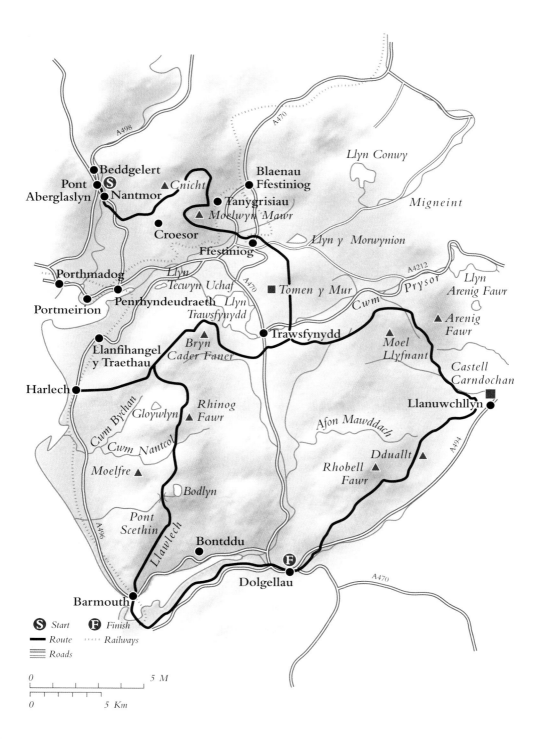

have been hurried. There are still alien creatures in Nantmor to maintain some part at least of Dafydd's tradition. I was once walking along the ancient path that traverses the west side of the valley when, most alarmingly, I ran into a llama, which eyeballed me from a distance of about two metres. I stood my ground while he came over to make a closer inspection; he tolerated my overtures of affection, which consisted of a tentative stroking of his muzzle, but soon decided that I was of no further interest. A flock of these animals is kept at Carneddi, the hill farm which the family of the writer Ruth Janette Ruck bought in 1945, and about which she wrote two of the best books in their genre, *Place of Stones* and *Hill Farm Story*.

The old track running east from Nantmor to Croesor is called the Roman Road. It's particularly lovely in the stretch where it crosses the Afon Dylif by a single-slab stone bridge. A path branches off to climb the south-west ridge of Cnicht. The name is simply the Anglo-Saxon version of our modern 'knight'; sailors in the estuary in early times are supposed to have bestowed the name for its resemblance to a Saxon knight's helmet, and it's odd that it has no Welsh counterpart. The stiff ascent up the south-west gable gives access to a sharp summit crest, and a view of fascinating country below: 'The dreary aspect and awful desolation of this extensive tract of hopeless sterility betrays no vestige of a dwelling, no mark of human footstep,' wrote the Reverend John Evans in 1798. Climb up to the top of Moelwyn Mawr – the next peak south – and you can trace his route, but the softness of these hills' name as you run it across your tongue belies his words: Moelwynion. I met an old man up here once, by Ceseiliau Duon on the old tramway that runs round the head of Maesgwm. It was a hot June day and his jacket was beside him on the glaciated bluff. He had a dark blue-grey scar three inches long from by his right ear-lobe to beneath his cheekbone, and the skin was tight and puckered around it like old parchment badly sewn. But his eyes were the blue of periwinkle flowers and his hands, set rigid into the grip a heavy hammer dictates, rolled a delicate cigarette, which he offered me. 'Moelwynion,' I said to him, 'means bare, white hills, doesn't it?'

'It could mean that,' he nodded, 'but my father always said it was corrupted from Moel yr Oen – the hill of the lamb – because from down in Tany-grisiau these hills looked to him like lambs skipping round each other in play.' He told me where he lived and invited me for a cup of tea if ever I passed by. I left him sitting there, capped and flannelled, with three inches of trouser waist above his belt, and never saw him again. For that November, when I did call, he was a month dead. 'The dust,' his widow explained in her small, crowded parlour, as she gave me delicate white cucumber sandwiches on her best china plates. 'The dust. I don't know how he got about in the hills with his lungs gone. Days when he couldn't get his breath. Pneumonia at the end, but it was the dust, see.'

The complex plateau between these hills and the heads of Cwm Orthin and Cwm Croesor is called Rhosydd. It has an effect on everyone who goes there. The dereliction, the strange displacement of former industry to a remote and mountainous setting seizes on the imagination. The glaciated ribs and bluffs are submerged within and the peaks themselves ride upon a sea of waste slate. Great rollers of spoil break upon its margins. The brilliant green of parsley fern drifts across it. Everything is going back, being re-absorbed; it is all finished, with the accomplished, long silence of a place that man has used and then abandoned. A window in a collapsed wall frames not the movement of sky but the earth's fixity, its capacity to heal – stonecrop spreads like the fibrous congealment of blood across a wound, moss and spleenwort softening the jag of discarded rock. The old tramway is grassed over and sags into the contours of the mountainside. People react differently to these industrial ruins in the hills. Some are repelled, insisting on the landscape's purity and primacy. Others immerse themselves in the task of imaginative reconstruction – a leat here, a supporting pylon there – and their minds tune to the thrum of past labour.

I always feel a terrible ambivalence. I love the sense of completion, of a moment having passed, but the waste and the exploitation of lives implicit in these ruins comes home to me: the smallness of barrack rooms, tiny fireplaces, the rough lime mortar pasted into cracked and seeping walls. These barracks at Rhosydd were a by-word for primitive conditions in an industry and at a time when the primitive was commonplace. Now, the place has become a part of our wealth. It has wildness, space, peace, resonance, surrounding beauty. Not for much longer, though. A proposal has been approved for the construction of a slate-waste road along the length of Cwm Orthin, and for the opencast quarrying of slate at Rhosydd. At its worst, this could mean that for sixty or seventy years 1000 tons of slate a week are brought by lorry down the quiet Cwm Orthin of the walkers and the anglers. The waters of the llyn will be clouded by dust and the shriek of diamond-saw cutters, which extract more rock in seven years than a massive work force of men could formerly have done in 200, will disturb the silence.

Should we object to a proposal that might bring more jobs, or at least maintain existing ones, in an area of high unemployment? I find myself, when faced by such dilemmas, torn by the differences of values and demands. I read the documents and reports that fly back and forth between developers and protesters and recognize the rhetoric, concealment, half-truths, selfishness, acquisitiveness and inability of either to acknowledge justice in the other's position. I see the sheer dogmatic unintelligence and lack of co-operation. I know about the national or ethnic element too. Once at a public inquiry I heard one of my own countrywomen stand up and hiss, 'It is our land and we will do what we want with it.' There is a darkness beyond civilization in that stance. Can we believe that the principles enshrined in the great legislation drafted in the late 1940s on the public utility of landscape will shine through and reflect light into the dark recesses of the Cwm Orthin debate? Do we have enough faith in human adaptability and ingenuity to believe that out of some of the arguments on the necessity

The conical peak of Cnicht dominates the skyline at the head of Cwm Croesor. Its name – the Anglo-Saxon for a knight – is supposed to have been given it by sailors in the estuary, from its fancied resemblance to a knight's helmet from those times.

to provide employment can come co-operative and imaginative enterprises? (Ffestiniog slate waste is transported 200 miles by road to a factory in South Wales to be pulverized and made into reconstituted high-quality slate-appearance roofing tiles, which sell for a fraction of the cost of their 'real' counterparts – why can this not be done on the spot?) I do know that Cwm Orthin and Rhosydd have a value to us seldom enumerated in the particularized paragraphs of developers and planners; it is a value not likely to attract the attention of Secretaries of State within whose gift the preservation of such places might ultimately lie, but whose devotion is to market forces, however unscrupulously those dark agents define themselves. Is not the land, and our relationship to it, in some subtle way at the centre of us? How we use it is crucial to the well-being of communities living around it now. How we leave it will be vital in terms of beauty and escape to generations to come. No one side has a monopoly on virtue in this argument.

The National Park has a hole in it called Blaenau Ffestiniog. The park boundary skirts fastidiously around its outskirts as though it were above mere industry. Blaenau's a slate town which people hate or love. I'm of the latter persuasion, but out of deference to others' feelings we'll pick our way down from the Moelwynion by ways that avoid it. Our route takes us across the Vale of Ffestiniog to the banks of the Afon Cynfal, where we re-encounter Lleu Llaw Gyffes's story, from *Math fab Mathonwy*. A destiny, you'll remember, was sworn upon Lleu Llaw Gyffes by his mother Aranrhod, that he would 'never have a wife of the race that is now on this earth'. When Lleu is a man, Gwydion the enchanter and Math the king create for him out of the flowers of meadowsweet, oak and broom the most beautiful woman, who is baptized Blodeuedd. Blodeuedd and Lleu marry, and Math gives them the lands of Eifionydd and Ardudwy, where they live together at Mur Castell. One day Lleu leaves Blodeuedd to visit Math. A hunt passes in his absence; at the dimming of the day, bloodied and tired, its members return past the court. Blodeuedd observes hospitality and invites them in. The leader is Gronw Bebyr, Lord of Penllyn:

Blodeuedd looked on him, and the moment she looked there was no part of her that was not filled with love of him. And he too gazed on her, and the same thought came to him as had come to her. He might not conceal that he loved her and he told her so. She knew great joy at heart. Nor did they delay longer than that night ere they embraced each other. And that night they slept together. (*The Mabinogion*, trans. by Thomas Jones and Gwyn Jones)

Gronw and Blodeuedd conspire to kill Lleu, who enjoys magical protection. She finds out in the privacy of their bedchamber how to accomplish his murder: there must be a bath on the bank of a river, framed over and thatched, Lleu standing with one foot on the rim, the other on the back of a billy-goat — only thus, and with a spear worked at through the course of a year only while people are at Mass on a Sunday, can he be killed. Blodeuedd sends word to Gronw. The spear is made. She prepares the bath under the lee of Bryn Cyfergyr on the bank of the Afon Cynfal, secures the goat, asks Lleu under pretence of fearing for his life to show her the position. Gronw conceals himself; Lleu raises his foot to the goat's back; the spear shears through his side. With a terrible scream, he flies away in the form of an eagle, leaving Gronw and Blodeuedd to hasten off to passion's bed.

But Math and Gwydion hear of the deed, and Gwydion searches through Gwynedd and Powys for the eagle. A sow leads him to the foot of a tree in Nantlle where she feeds on the maggots and rotten flesh that rain down from an eagle in the topmost branches. Gwydion lures the bird down, restores it to the form of Lleu and nurses him back to health at the court of Math. Together they muster a force of armed men and set out for Mur Castell to seek redress. Blodeuedd hears of their coming and flees across the

OVERLEAF The Afon Serw flows through the wide moors of the Migneint under the slopes of Arenig Fawr. The textural beauty of this spacious, wind-rippled, curlew-haunted and unfrequented region changes subtly season to season as the heathers and moor-grasses bloom and fade.

mountains with her handmaidens. Looking behind them out of fear, they fall into a lake, now called Llyn y Morwynion, where all drown with the exception of Blodeuedd, whom Gwydion turns into an owl, bird of night and lonely voice. For Gronw Bebyr, that which he gave he must now receive. He stands in the place where Lleu stood when the spear was cast, to take the blow in his turn. But he asks whether he might interpose a stone between himself and the spear's flight, since he was led to this pass by a woman's wiles. The request is granted, the stone raised, the warrior's arm draws back, his eye glittering on its target. The spear sails, pierces stone and flesh, breaks the deceiver's spine, and the story ends with these words: *'Ac yna y llas Gronw Bebyr, ac yno y mae y llech ar lan Afon Cynfal yn Ardudwy, a'r twll drwydi. Ac o achos hynny eto y galwir Llech Gronw.'* (And so Gronw Bebyr was slain, and there the stone is on the bank of Afon Cynfal in Ardudwy, and the hole through it. And because of that, it is still called Llech Gronw.)

The stone still exists, but is not easy to find. It lies prone in a drift of oak-leaves with earth at the back of its terrible eye, the story perhaps an explanation of a much older site, of which the quartz and shaped stones scattered around are remains. Beyond it, the old road Sarn Helen leads up to the Roman military base of Tomen y Mur – the Mur Castell of the story – a complex and confusing site, much of it on private land, with medieval castle fortifications overlying the earlier defensive works. Two miles further on, the road arrives at the straggling, upland village of Trawsfynydd. Apart from its sacrilegious nuclear power station, this little moorland place is most famous as home to the poet Hedd Wyn (Ellis Evans) who won the Chair at the Birkenhead Eisteddfod of 1917 for his *awdl 'Yr Arwr'* ('The Hero'). With the award came the announcement that he had died a month before at the battle of Pilkem Ridge. The Chair was draped in black, the eisteddfod thereafter known as *'Eisteddfod Gadair Ddu'* ('Eisteddfod of the Black Chair'). There is a statue to him in the village, and a recent film on his life was Oscar-nominated in the 'best foreign film' category. He was thirty years old when he died, and had been in France for only two months. His family's farm is

Yr Ysgwrn in Cwm Prysor, and the last poem he wrote – a quatrain found among his papers in France – is simply called *'Atgof'* ('Recollection'):

Dim ond lleuad borffor
Ar ffin y mynydd llwm;
A sŵn hen afon Prysor
Yn canu yn y Cwm.

(Nothing but the purple moon/On the end of the leaden mountain/ And sound of the old river Prysor/Singing in the Cwm.)

Moon and mountain also figure large in the work of a very different artist working in this area at the time of Hedd Wyn's early successes in local eisteddfodau. One night in 1910, John Dickson Innes came to the lonely inn of Rhyd y Fen, at the head of Cwm Prysor, and when he saw the twin-peaked Arenig Fawr rising above next morning, he was enthralled. He returned next spring with Augustus John, who wrote of him that his 'passionate love of Wales was the supreme mainspring of his art and though he worked much in the south of France Mynydd Arenig remained his sacred mountain and the slopes of Migneint his spiritual home.' John and Innes shared for a time the small cottage of Amnodd Wen in the valley between Arenig and Moel Llyfnant; while Innes was here, he buried on the summit of the mountain a packet of love-letters for which art historians, would-be biographers and prurient gossips have hunted in vain. They probably burnt or were scattered to the four winds when an American Flying Fortress bomber crashed here in 1943 with the loss of its eight crew members. There is a memorial to them at the summit, and aircraft bits still lie around. Innes himself died of tuberculosis in 1914 at the age of twenty-seven.

The path past Amnodd Wen leads over a shallow pass beneath Arenig and down into the green and quiet valley of the Afon Lliw. Small, elegant chapels testify to its former population, but the tide of humanity has been receding for a century and more, and only a froth of holiday visitors and a craggy remnant of indigenous farming stock people it now. On the north of the

NESTA WYN JONES

'We tend to know who even the third cousins are,' confides the brown-eyed woman sitting opposite me in the shadowy farm-house kitchen. 'That's rare these days.' To back up the statement, her conversation ranges over genealogies: distant relationship to Hedd Wyn ('but then, everyone round here claims kinship with him'); the names of the farms, the occupa- tions ('He came over with the threshing machine and married the daughter at Penstryd') of her people in this valley for the last 300 years, their line plotted back to the fourteenth century ('and then we were only in Bala, so we've not come far'); the help and interest from Tecwyn Lloyd, pioneer of adult and continuing education in rural Wales and celebrant of its community values.

She goes on to tell of how much easier life now is in Abergeirw, with the telephone and the deep freeze, the snow-ploughs along the improved roads in winter so that they've not been cut off for more than two days in years, and the generator giving light (there's no mains electricity yet to the farmhouse where she lives with her mother – 'my other memory' – her husband Gwilym and thirteen-year-old daughter Annest. Her ninety-two-year-old grandmother's house is only two miles away). But with progress comes loss too. The close-knit society of former years has changed, perhaps irrevocably. She brings out photographs: two brothers and a sister, aged, by the hearth at the old farm of Twr y Maen two miles up-valley, which has gone now beneath the conifers ('it's not true that only poor land was used – they planted on hayfields where I used to play as a child'); its family dying one by one, the last of them, Ifan, in Wrexham. In the photograph, rough clothes, strong faces, and yet lined and permeated with humour, strength, gravity. They bring alive for me Alan Llwyd's resonant line, *'Bywyd gwâr mewn bŷd gerwin'* (A civilized life in a harsh world). And Nesta, too, reminds me of it as she sketches the activity taken as subject in one of her best-known poems, *'Pluo gwyddau'* ('Plucking Geese'), a light in her eyes and her face all animated and lovely as she paints detail – the little pile of snow blown under the door, the great mound of feathers, the red flame and the flickering conversation of former years.

For this farmer over 555 acres of hill, this shepherd to 500 breeding ewes, is also the most accomplished woman poet of modern Wales, Chair of *Yr Academi Gymreig* (Welsh academy), is part – and a significant one at that – of the nation's cultural stock. She tells me of her days at Dr Williams's School in Dolgellau; of a teacher, Brenda Wyn Jones, who stayed, unlike most young women who soon moved on, and encouraged her in all the different forms of poetry; of how she, Nesta, used poetry to bring into her life some sense of order, some understanding of the confusion: religious crisis, language and loss, love affairs, praise for the mentors.

She speaks of her poem *'Cysgodion'* ('Shadows'), written after watching a documentary on the history of the Jews. Her words flow on: over the names of her own square mile – Hendreberfedd, Beddycoedwr, Hafod-fraith; over the stories her great-grandfather wrote down, of the ghost of a hare with traces and chains, of a white fairy bull; over her own lament for this fine place that the ignorant would deem desolate. 'The way of life I remember – it has changed so radically since the 1960s.'

As we stand outside – she holding in large, strong hands with such love the last of a line of calm, bright dogs; she standing on the plunging slope, a slim, strong woman with the red-gold glint in her hair; she gazing at the trees gaunt by ruins above – her lines are crying in my memory: *'Na, ni wyddom ni ddim am y dyddiau hynny,/Dim ond clywed weithiau/Am ryw ddigwyddiadau y tu hwnt i ddeall/Cyn ein hamser ni'* (No, we know nothing about those days/Except to hear sometimes/Of things beyond understanding/From before our time).

The scales in which atrocity and civilization are weighed have many degrees, their fulcrum the fine, pained balance of a poet's mind.

river a road weaves its way over spur and marsh to come down eventually to Trawsfynydd. South of the river and a-bob with grey wagtails, the road from Llanuwchllyn merges into a track beneath the rocky bluff on top of which is mysterious Castell Carndochan. There must once have been a castle of sorts here, though all that remain now on the summit are wall-footings of dressed stone and traces of rough lime mortar from which spleenwort, as ever, grows. The only historical reference to it is in the posthumously published work of an attractive character, Richard Fenton, the eighteenth-century Welsh topographical writer and friend of Johnson and Goldsmith, who visited in 1798. He suggests the place must have been 'refuge of some ferocious chief who had lost all claim to society and who lived by plunder and rapine.'

Upstream, a path climbs through spruce plantation to a marshy *bwlch*, or pass. In front, Dduallt (the Black Height) lifts into view; beneath it is one of the powerful places in the Welsh hills, but one to which few people ever go. It's called Waun y Griafolen, which means 'moor of the rowan tree', although there are no rowans here now. If you go down among the peat groughs of this raised bog, their embedded remains are clear enough. Its surface area is about two miles long by a mile wide, and it lies in a basin surrounded on all sides, except the one on which Dduallt rears up, by low ridges. It is wonderfully spacious and empty. The heathers, rushes, mosses and grasses have simply taken over, obliterated all and started again in their slow way. An attempt's been made to drain the area, and ditches cross it regularly, for more forestry, no doubt, which would be a manifest obscenity here. But the ditches too, futile as they are, are being filled in as frond, tendril and blossom uncurl, straighten toward the sun, bend in the wind, fall, rot, and compact down to sustain this simple place. The path marked as crossing it is conceptual rather than actual. Among the preserved rowan stumps are the smoothed rocks of old passage, but it has been erased, and the line shown on the map would be dangerous to follow. The Afon Mawddach drains out in deep canals from the reed-choked former pool of Llyn Crych y Waen.

Better to describe a prudent ellipse, avoiding the brightest green moss and heading for the obvious step low on the north ridge of Dduallt. When I was here last, cloud from which I'd been freed spread down the valley of the Dee towards England. Peaks were islanded among it, and all around were the hills of Wales, clear and identifiable. Frost flowered the moss beneath the summit, where two grey falcons perched on rocks, watching. I was bound for the neighbouring peak of Rhobell Fawr, one of our prime hills, from which on a clear day you can see from Snowdon in the north to Pumlumon in the south, from Garn Fadryn to the west to Caer Caradoc in Shropshire. I made my way sunwise down this 'noble mountain', as Patrick Monkhouse terms it, after half a mile or so picking up the path that runs down to the Bwlch Goriwared. The sun set in the estuary of the river whose birthplace I'd traversed and in the afterlight, on a cushion of emerald moss, lay a corona of pearl-grey down and feathers with a splash of bright blood at its centre – a peregrine's kill, fresh and savagely beautiful, the peace of the hills stilling it now, night fading its violence, the falcon chattering distantly on its rock, the long bulk of Cadair Idris in front acid-etched against a tangerine-and-eggshell sky and the welcoming lights of Dolgellau beneath.

If, instead of heading east from Trawsfynydd, we trek round to the far side of the lake, a very different country lies ahead. Redundant pylons (why cannot they now be removed?) from the defunct power station strut through its northern edge and over the salt-flats by Penrhyndeudraeth to defile the most beautiful of Welsh estuaries, that of the Dwyryd. Pilgrims in the Middle Ages needed guides to cross this from Llanfihangel y Traethau above, on their way by the Taith y Pererin (Pilgrims' Way) to Ynys Enlli, and at low tide if you are daring you can do the same. The sense of danger adds piquancy to the vast sense of space, whose allurement draws you in. You must time your

OVERLEAF Of all Welsh hills, none are rougher and rockier than the Rhinogydd, which form a barrier between the eastern moorland and the central plain of Ardudwy. This harsh and punishing terrain is nonetheless jewelled with exquisite lakes and intersected by winding valleys of sylvan loveliness.

visit cautiously. Slack water here turns with inexorable rapidity. The channel between you and the shore carried no more than a trickle moments ago. There is a hissing and suddenly it is a deep, black flood, widening, bubbling, spilling over the tidal flats. In a space of minutes you can be cut off, with no option but to swim through treacherous currents.

This is an enthralling place for bird-watchers. Curlews gather in great flocks, gliding down in wheeling formation on sandbanks or coastal fields with graceful, droop-winged flight. At night you hear their bubbling, whistling, chuckling song until one soloist pitches up to the crescendo and every other bird's call cascades after. Flocks of pintail, exquisitely elegant and several thousand strong, occupy islands in the huge expanses of shallow water where two rivers meet, and where tide has sculpted the estuarine sand into lyrical texture and curve. Barnacle geese take off, advance in ragged skeins to land upstream among the saltings, where they graze and querulously scold passing sheep. Smaller birds move quietly about their business; dunlin stitch their patient trail hunch-shouldered along the tideline; oyster-catchers with dapper scurry and piping flight race each other to draining eddies where handfuls of mussels are washed up. And from the bank, Clough Williams-Ellis's fantasy village of Portmeirion looks jauntily on, like a child in fancy dress, sweet, self-conscious, pleased with itself.

Our path traverses the hillside high above, its turf a soft and springy green. Where the rock strata of the mountain rake across it, they are worn smooth. We are making our way through the *rhiniogau* (the thresholds) of the Rhinogydd, the most rough, wild and strange group of hills in the whole of the mountainous country of Wales. That word 'Rhinog' itself prompts a small essay on character of place. Ifor Williams, in his *Enwau Lleoedd* ('Names of Places', the standard work on Welsh toponymy) has it as a corruption or elision of *yr hiniog* (the threshold) and I don't think that those who first gave this name to the rough hills that separate Harlech and Ardudwy from the valleys leading to England had their merely physical characteristic as a barrier in mind. There is something *rhiniol* – secret, mysterious, even otherworldly – about them. They are not simple, smooth-flanked, upright and open as other hills are. They are harsh, primal. I came with my son William when he was seven or eight into this most complex landscape, an area of tiny crags and knolls and brief marshy valleys with no obvious orientation. The cloud was low, our focus restricted to jewels of dew on the red blades of the moor grass, mist-wraiths swirling round us, and all around us too was evidence of the place's former inhabitants: a fragment of low field-wall descending into the bog; a pile of burnt, particular stone by a pit; a ring-cairn alongside the trackway. Each of these was accentuated by the mist-closed horizons, and so powerfully atmospheric that William became scared by their mystery and stole his hand into mine for reassurance. We crossed the head of Nant Pasgan, where there is a house – blind-windowed, lifeless, boarded up – which is the best preserved, and in Clough Williams-Ellis's view the most beautiful, medieval dwelling in Snowdonia. It's owned by a consortium of families from Cambridge who spend a week or two holidaying in it each year. A few hundred metres farther, and in clear weather you have your first view of Bryn Cader Faner.

The archaeologist Frances Lynch describes the site as 'a monument of simple but brilliantly effective design, placed with sophisticated precision in its dramatic setting so as to achieve maximum impact on travellers approaching from the south. It is arguably the most beautiful Bronze Age monument in Britain.' I share her enthusiasm. The silhouette of its outward-pointing stones is crown-like and has an intimate majesty perfectly in harmony with the cyclopean masonry of its natural setting. It was here 2000 years before the birth of Christ and its resonance and artistry remain. Travellers through four millennia respected it. Before the war, it was acknowledged as the

OVERLEAF High on a ridge in the rough bounds of the Rhinogydd, its silhouette crown-like as you approach from the south, lies Bryn Cader Faner, 'arguably the most beautiful Bronze Age monument in Britain'. Once perfectly preserved, it was severely damaged by soldiers on a training exercise at the beginning of the Second World War.

best-preserved Bronze Age monument in Snowdonia. And yet soldiers training here on an exercise at the outbreak of the Second World War half-destroyed it. Although the silhouette is unaffected, to the north and east its great stones have been pulled out and scattered mindlessly.

The ancient trackway we've followed from Trawsfynydd, its verges studded with cairns, standing stones, settlements and field systems, continues from Bryn Cader Faner to Mochras, and the temptation to follow it down to Harlech is strong. The opening of the second branch of the *Mabinogi*, *Branwen Ferch Llyr*, takes place in Harlech – the name derives from *hardd lech* (beautiful rock) – and if you're already acquainted with the rugged terrain across these northern summits of the Rhinogydd, the call of the town, with its supremely romantic castle, associations with Owain Glyndŵr, and the Hotel Plas conservatory cafe, which has the best view from any such establishment in Britain, may well prove irresistible. But there are easier paths at a lower level contouring round into Cwm Bychan, from which a paved medieval packhorse trail ('The Roman Steps') climbs back over the Bwlch Tyddiad towards Abergeirw. A mile south of Cwm Bychan is Gloywlyn, the bright lake, which comes with the best references:

> ...this is my country, beloved by me best,
> The first land that rose from Chaos and the Flood,
> Nursing no valleys for comfort or rest.

That's how Robert Graves saw the 'rocky acres' where it lies, in what he claims was 'the first poem I wrote as myself', going on to tell how he found here a 'personal peace independent of history or geography'; how 'wherever we went the rocky skeleton of the hill seemed only an inch or two beneath the turf' in 'this country (and I know no country like it)', which 'seemed independent of formal nature'. He came to Gloywlyn to gather cranberries in the wild innocence of his youth, before the Great War caused him to bid goodbye to all that. The natural history writer William Condry has been here too, and offers up this prayer in what for me is the finest of all books written about the Welsh hills: 'Gloywlyn...lies close under the backbone of the Rhinog. Long may it remain, unexploited, tranquil and remote, for the spirit of man needs such retreats.'

The two miles over the western spur of Rhinog Fawr from Gloywlyn to Maes y Garnedd seem like five through boulder and heather. Maes y Garnedd, the topmost farm in Cwm Nantcol, was the birthplace, in about 1597, of a man who is invariably referred to as 'John Jones the Regicide'. It is certainly true that John Jones was one of the fifty-nine signatories to the death warrant of the despotic and disastrous Charles I. It is also true that he was a brave and honourable soldier, a humane and highly principled republican who became Cromwell's brother-in-law and served on his Council of State, and a man of sincere and charitable religious conviction. At the Restoration, excluded from the general amnesty, he was hanged, drawn and quartered by those whom Milton termed 'the mad multitude, in their besotted and degenerate baseness of spirit'. The last glimpse history has of him is from Pepys's diary, where, in the entry for 17 October 1660, the diarist encounters Jones's 'still smoking limbs' being carried victoriously through the streets of London by a mob whose descendants would no doubt have done the same to Michael Foot had Margaret Thatcher required it.

Cwm Nantcol has a tiny Independent chapel at its head. People confuse this with the Baptist chapel of Salem much lower down the valley, in which Curnow Vosper painted his famous 1909 study of an old lady in traditional dress, prints of which used to hang on the wall of most Welsh homes, my grandmother's included. The picture is highly sentimentalized – it was later used as a soap advertisement and the original is now in the Lever Gallery in Port Sunlight. This higher, Independent chapel with its schoolroom and tiny

OVERLEAF What forces brought together, arranged, all the component parts of the scene? What blessing of sunlight was bestowed upon them, blasts of gale hurled against them, through times beyond our notation? Polished by the raven's foot, light and disposable to the Earth's powers, they assert their presence, fixed only in our brief consciousness.

schoolmaster's house, built from the grey gleaming rock of the mountain and anchored in its bare ribs, is a finer, holier place. To sit in its quiet garden among the hills on a February afternoon, with stray shafts of sunlight piercing the clouds, illuminating like the most perfect praise-text stands of short early daffodils, a palpable testimony of value and belief embodied in these raised-up stones, is at least a glimpse of a glimpse of heaven; it brings with it a certain joy and strength that enable you almost to cope with the atrocities committed against things you love.

Just over the shoulder of Moelfre from Cwm Nantcol in the southern Rhinogydd is Pont Scethin, a bridge in one of the most fragile and exquisite landscapes of a country of exquisite and fragile natural beauty.

Even the statutory bodies have recognized its distinction: in 1979 a huge acreage, with Pont Scethin at its centre, was designated an 'Ancient Landscape'. It is, in the words of Peter Crew, the National Park's archaeologist, 'the most important area archaeologically in Wales, and stands comparison with any in Britain. The valley has an exceptional range of relict features, of which Pont Scethin is only the most obvious.' On a bright January day nine years ago I was bound for a picnic by Pont Scethin, filled with pleasurable anticipation. This is what I found. At the point where you cross the spur that ends in the Iron Age fort of Craig y Ddinas, and where the old road to Pont Scethin leaves the new track which the Welsh Water Authority in its wisdom has forced through to the high mountain lake of Bodlyn, a great mound of alien aggregate had been dumped on the green moorgrass, dwarfing the standing stone that marks the old route. From here to 100 metres the other side of Pont Scethin, the green track had been transformed to a quagmire in places fifty metres wide. Rock strata breaking through the smooth surface of the moor and ground to a fine sheen by long-departed ice had been crushed and shattered by the caterpillar tracks of JCBs, to ease the progress of which more aggregate had been scattered about. Another load had been dumped by the abutments of little Pont Scethin; concrete had been mixed there, litter and broken glass scattered about and drums of lubricant discarded, with some hurled into the pure, rapid stream. A rough ford had been made, breaking down the stream's green banks and reducing them to mud, which washed down continually. A hundred metres beyond, in a great hole dug there, was a shiny tank with stop-cocks and pipework. All this was in the hasty cause of upgrading an industry at public expense before it was sold off to greedy individual speculators and even greedier City financiers.

After I had recovered from the psychological devastation this scene wrought upon me, I wrote an article entitled 'The Clear Sight of Janet Haigh' (there is a memorial stone above Pont Scethin whose inscription reads: *'Gogoniant i Dduw*. To the enduring memory of Janet Haigh, who even as late as her 84th year, despite dim sight and stiffened joints, still loved to walk this way from Talybont to Penmaenpool. "Courage, Traveller"'). My article excoriated the politicians and developers whose ill-favoured schemes so harm the spiritual resource that is landscape. After it had been published I sent it, along with a dossier of photographs, to the chairman of the Welsh Water Authority. To his considerable credit, he disciplined the planners in his own authority whose laxity had enabled this outrage to take place, and he ordered immediate work to restore the landscape as nearly as possible to its former state. It is too fragile, of course, for this restitution to be entirely effective within our lifetimes. But at least an effort that went considerably beyond the merely token was made, at least the head of Welsh Water had the moral courage to assume responsibility for what had been done in his name, and take positive action to remedy it.

An old stagecoach road climbs from Pont Scethin and crosses the grassy, quiet ridge of Llawlech, but to imagine horses pulling coaches up this rocky, steep pass almost beggars belief. Bwlch y Rhiwgyr, two miles to the south, is one of the drovers' ways from the fattening lands of Ardudwy, Eifionydd and Lleyn to the English smithfields. I had little trouble when I was last here imagining the surge and racket, shouting and hallooing of herd and riders going through the narrow pass to their next night-stop at Bontddu or Dolgellau. A few minutes later my imaginings became reality, as a frisking

SIAN ROBERTS

Elfin-faced, animated, she sits at a table in the
sunshine outside her cafe in Coed y Brenin as
the resiny scent of the pines distils into the gathering cool of evening. She sparkles with enthusiasm.
Her topic's the house she and her partner Dafydd
own, centuries old and on an ancient religious site
between the great raised bog of Crawcwellt and
the infant meanders of the Afon Eden. Its continuing restoration is their winter project, when the
cafe closes down at the end of October and the
walkers, the mountain-bikers, the motor-bound

tourists who provide their seasonal living all ebb
away. She's researched every detail of its history,
checked them out in the archives down in Dolgellau, knows the names of its inhabitants down the
generations, even the age of the three great yews
which protect it from the west wind and once sig-
nalled pasture and shelter for the cattle drovers
whose herds lowed and leaped and bellowed this
way, bound for the smithfields of England. She has
that rootedness about her, the fierce determination
to take her stand here and the pride in her own

country – as when she talks of having rescued this house from the desolation of holiday-cottage use – which seem typically and appropriately Welsh.

Yet Sian Roberts was not always so sure and confident about identity and direction. She talks of her schooldays at Ysgol Ardudwy, which came to an end less in a firm act of leaving than in drifting out of the schoolroom and on to the dole, then short-term contracts labouring in the forestry plantations, not knowing what to do in an area where opportunities for permanent employment were scant ('Tourism is run by English people with the capital to set up in business; the Welsh get the cooking and cleaning jobs'), and futures were construed in terms of academic achievement and moving away. She might have gone the way of many contemporaries, caught in the spiral of early pregnancy, poor housing, abusive relationships, benefit-dependency.

Instead, and unexpectedly for someone who'd shown no interest in games at school, the vitality of her character found its expression in a sport. At the age of nineteen she took up running, started to win fell-races – you sense there are no half-measures with this woman, that the dedication's an absolute – and found work promoting games she'd hated at school for *Cyngor Chwaraeon Cymru* (the Welsh Sports Council).

That came to an abrupt end. Running up Tryfan in training one day, she experienced crippling pain in a hip joint, chronic bursitis was diagnosed, and one career was over. Rather than sit down and cry over it, with two friends and five old mountain-bikes she set up *Beics Betws*, a bike-hire business run initially from an old shed behind the Tan Lan bakery in Betws y Coed. At the outset she didn't even know how to ride a bike; within a year she was established in the new sport of mountain-bike racing, and winning there too.

She talks with enthusiasm about her early days, about the wild careering along rocky forest tracks solely for the joy of the thing. The flicker of a shadow passes over her clear blue eyes and she moves on to tell of the disciplines of the modern sport at which she came to excel: never a ride for simple pleasure any more, each time she mounts a bike it's for a training bout, heart-rate monitor attached, three-hour sessions of aerobic-capacity work at least once a day – hard, scientific, intense. In post-Thatcher Britain, even play takes on the structures and vocabulary of work.

So at thirty-two, this voluble, lovely young woman with the wavy brown hair, lithe physique, solid forearms and thick, strong fingers, has found it impossible to reconcile the demands of a full-time job and international sporting competition. To continue in the latter she would have had to turn professional and dedicate herself to it entirely. Now, she's dropped herself from the British Olympic team, is heart and soul into the new venture. Her and her partner's cafe and bike-hire business is at the visitor centre in Coed y Brenin, franchised from Forest Enterprise in the middle of a great tract of land whose designated theme is to be mountain biking. An international-standard competition circuit's been laid out here and the first race is to be held next year. She, Dafydd and Llwyd the dog won't go far – this, after all, is their home – but from the energy Sian brings even to the simple task of tonight's four-hour baking session to cater for consumption in the cafe tomorrow, you know they'll do well.

frenzy of impressively horned bullocks came bellowing and careering down the road, followed by a darting, diminutive Irishman intent on whacking them as often as possible across their hindquarters with a stout cudgel – hence the noise. After him, a whiskery, intelligent-looking gentleman of a certain age pulled up alongside me in a car, cast a few appraising glances and interrogative remarks in my direction, ascertained what I was up to and then invited me to step inside the next house along the road for coffee. Given the opportunity of an attentive guest, Mr Tony Turner, as he introduced himself, then delivered himself of the following monologue: born into the gentry, but small gentry, not rich, farmed in Nova Scotia and Oregon before he came here fifteen years ago, essentially a peasant farmer, scraping by in this rocky, hard place, but a *working* farmer – he was at pains to stress that to me, but I knew it anyway from the rough-skinned grasp of his hand; chairman of the Country Landowners' Association in these parts but a member of environmental bodies too, although some of the unprincipled careerists in that field, with their knee-jerk oppositional responses were not entirely to his taste; worried about the direction of the country – yes, he was a Tory, had been all his life, but this lot! He was in favour of the old-style Labour policies of 95 per cent Supertax for dealing with their greed, self-interest and evasions; would never vote Tory again, and what good was Europe for the farmer – for the *real* farmer, as opposed to these never-get-their-hands-dirty acre-millionaires who cared nothing for, were effectively ruining, the land that had nurtured him and to which he was, he hoped, returning that trust and care? I left him, as he was on his way to church, and carried on down towards Barmouth musing on how much common ground, once you start talking, is to be found between a sparky, hospitable and altruistic paternalist Old High Tory like the good Mr Turner, and someone like myself, committed to a political creed apparently entirely different and at odds.

Those people to whom I mention my enthusiasm for Barmouth generally assume the cautious expression you wear when dealing with the mentally unbalanced, and round on me asking how I can possibly like 'that dump, that Black Country vacational sink estate'. It does have about it elements of the shabby patience and desperate bright vulgarity of a seaside haunt gone out of fashion. But to me the place is entrancing. For a start it has among its stacked and jumbled terraces some very good pubs with very good beer. After a long day on the ridges, walking into the sun, easing and ambling your way seawards along their final grassy heights, you reach them as you should reach a town's attractions – by secretive little stepped paths and alleyways dropping off the ridge with teasing views of the resort's magnificent setting, disposed along the headland under which the Mawddach escapes to the sea. And then there are the associations: with Ruskin and the grandiose Victorian idealism of the Guild of St George; with Fanny Talbot, the benign friend of Canon Rawnsley and Octavia Hill, two of the three founders of the National Trust. Mrs Talbot gave a four-and-a-half acre enclosure on the hill called Dinas Oleu (the Fortress of Light) directly above the town, so that the poor and the ordinary people of the place might have a 'beautiful sitting room in which to take pleasure and delight'. It was the Trust's first acquisition and remains lovingly tended, special, and in their care. Mrs Talbot also gave a home to the exiled French radical journalist Auguste Guyard, friend of Hugo, Dumas and Lamartine, and lovers of the curious will seek out his grave plot with its odd inscription among these selfsame alleys and pathways above the town. For me, Barmouth's main attraction is its association with H. W. Tilman, who lived here from the 1930s until he left on his final voyage in the summer of 1977. The times I visited him, the conversations with this most remarkable of explorers and mountain writers, even the running of errands for him to the town's wholefood store, remain as indelible and precious as when they first took place. They certainly figured large in my memories as I paid my thirty pence at the toll-booth, crossed the wooden promenade alongside the railway bridge over the estuary, and walked the few miles of old track to Dolgellau. But more of that in the next chapter.

CHAPTER FIVE

MARGINS

Dolgellau is the oddest little town, piled-up and intricate, consistent in its grey stone and plain, elegant style, and peered down on by the summit crags of Mynydd Moel, easternmost of the trinity of peaks that make up Cadair Idris. The architect Henry Wilson, writing in 1895, obviously appreciated the place:

> What is so beautiful in Dolgelley [the old spelling of the town's name] seen from the hill on the station side of the river is the sense of appropriateness, of rightness in the arrangement of slate roofs and grey and white walls. When the eye passes from the town to Cader Idris or the surrounding hills and slopes, one feels that there is a sort of family likeness, a relationship between the works of man and his maker.

Spending time here in pubs and cafes, procrastinating in the National Milk Bar (an institution in every town in North and Mid-Wales), listening to the playful conversation and admiring the lovely faces of the local young women before setting out for the summits is a very pleasant pastime, and one favoured by the Reverend Francis Kilvert – surely the most amiable of all our great diarists – who did much the same thing in 1871:

> I was very much struck and taken with the waitress at the Golden Lion. She said her name was Jane Williams and that her home was at Bettws y Coed.

Penygadair, high point of the Cadair Idris ridge.

> She was a beautiful girl with blue eyes, eyes singularly lovely, the sweetest saddest most weary and most patient eyes I ever saw. It seemed as if she had a great sorrow in her heart. Into the soup the cook had upset both the salt cellar and the pepper box.

Kilvert seemed determined to have fun during his stay in Dolgellau. Wombwell's menagerie was in town, and on the day he climbed Cadair Idris, he rose at 5.30 a.m. to take a look:

> The people were all asleep, but the lions were rustling and growling about their dens hungry for breakfast. The caravans were full of strange noises of the different beasts. I knocked at the lions' door and at the doors of the ostriches, gnus and antelopes, eliciting divers roars, groans, howls, hoots and grunts.

Kilvert's guide took him up Cadair by way of the Pony Track, which gains the ridge at Bwlch Rhiw Gwredydd, west of the summit. It's still the most popular ascent, but the path that climbs Fron Serth — the name means 'steep hill', and it is precisely that — on the outskirts of town, leads into an exquisite region of oakwoods, sheep pasture and little ridges at the north-eastern end of the Cadair range looking out to Rhobell Fawr, which from this angle rises with an attractive symmetry above the valley of the Wnion. You pick up the old, flagged pony track over to the top of the Tal y Llyn pass, and follow it across marshy hollows, where a rare and, it has to be said rather nondescript little plant, the bog orchid, grows — to gain the eastern bulwark of what is perhaps the longest and finest mountain ridge south of the Scottish border. The ascent to its first summit, Gau Graig, is a merciless climb, the view opening out to the north and east with every metre gained. There is a steep and gravelly further ascent from Gau Graig up to the ridge's next tier at Mynydd Moel. From the state of the paths, by far the greater number who climb Cadair seem never to venture so far as Mynydd Moel, which is a great hill in its own right, massive in presence as you approach it from the east. Its top is particularly fine, with a shelter-cairn and a little

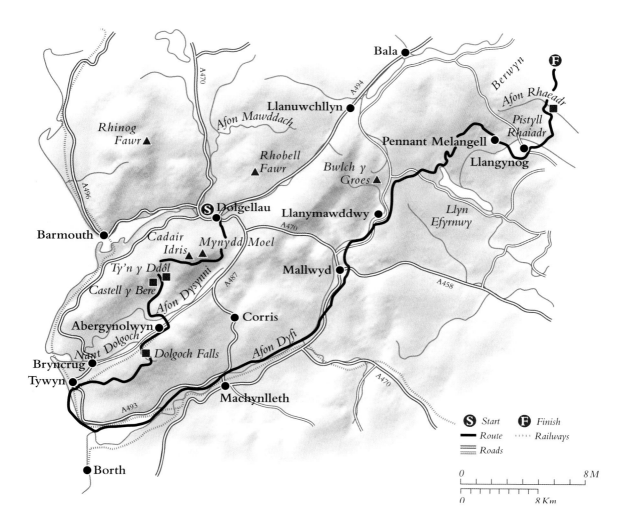

Bala

Berwyn

Afon Rhaeadr

F

Pistyll
Rhaiadr

Llanuwchllyn

Afon Mawddach

Pennant Melangell

Llangynog

Rhinog
Fawr ▲

Rhobell
Fawr ▲

Bwlch y
Groes ▲

Llyn
Efyrnwy

Dolgellau S

Llanymawddwy

A470

Barmouth

Cadair
Idris

Mynydd Moel

Ty'n y Ddôl

Afon Dysynni

Castell y Bere

Mallwyd

A458

Abergynolwyn

A487

Corris

Afon Dyfi

Nant Dolgoch

Dolgoch Falls

Bryncrug

Tywyn

A493

Machynlleth

A470

Borth

S Start   F Finish
━━ Route   ⋯⋯ Railways
≣ Roads

0   8 M

0   8 Km

cockscomb of rocks above plunging crags. You can see straight down on to Dolgellau, scarcely two miles away, which gives you a clue as to why, in Elizabethan times, this was considered the highest mountain in the British Isles. Penygadair, the highest point of the Cadair range, may be only 893 metres above sea level, but sea level is just down there; Dolgellau is at it. Ben Nevis is half as high again, but it is twice as far from the sea. The sand-flats and saltings of the Mawddach estuary give Cadair its uplift, its subjective impression of height – it *feels* a tremendous mountain. And I'm tempted to state that Mynydd Moel is the best part of it. Even its name suggests the effect it has, translating loosely as *'the mountain mountain'* in a deliberately intensifying way. From it, you look right along the northern escarpment, lakes flashing silver from glaciated hollows around which elegant ridges glint skywards. Walk a few metres down the southern slope and you're confronted by memory of a masterpiece of eighteenth-century art.

Richard Wilson's 'Cader Idris, Llyn-y-cau' of 1765 is one of those paintings which anyone with a vestige of interest in art knows. It's in the Tate Gallery in London, and is a surprisingly small canvas, not much more than about forty-five centimetres high by sixty centimetres wide, all muted reds and Payne's gray with the palest blues and greens and a touch of gold on foreground boulders rooting its conceptual diagonals firmly in the landscape. The painting always shocks me with its capacity simultaneously to be like and yet unlike. It's less the depiction of a mountain scene than its re-ordering, the interpretation of its essence by a man with a kindly, respectful and loving view of nature and its power for harmony.

If Richard Wilson had seen a day like the one in December when I was last here, his painting might have been even more haunting and suffused

PREVIOUS PAGES The Ffordd Ddu – the black road – runs all along the northern scarp of Cadair Idris, its course marked and punctuated by an exceptional concentration of burial monuments, standing stones and settlements, at their most numerous in the vicinity of Llynnau Gregennan, near which this fine megalith is to be found.

with the golden light of a Claude landscape, instead of containing its merest suggestion. I've seldom seen so far from the hills: to the north, Snowdon seemed almost within touching distance, and Snaefell hung like a cloud behind it, whilst to the south-east and the south-west the Malvern Hills and the Preselis delimited the horizon, so clear their every summit was identifiable. Only to the west was the clarity compromised by a heavy front, which moved inexorably in through the course of the afternoon. A blustery wind scoured the plateau between Mynydd Moel and Penygadair. Two walkers surfing along on it stopped to talk excitedly of the day's quality, their speech gasping and fragmented: 'Perfect...the views...can see everything!' I left them to climb on to the summit, and all the memories that place holds.

It was here, twenty years ago, that one of the most remarkable and all-too-brief friendships of my life began. With my labrador bitch, a seasoned winter mountaineer, I'd climbed the banked-out snow-gully that leads directly to the summit on the north side of Cadair Idris. There is a shelter just below the cairn – a low stone hut built of boulders with tiny windows, a corrugated-iron roof and wooden benches inside. We crept into it out of the wind. I put down my ice-axes, unstrapped my crampons, gave the dog some biscuits for reward, and took out my flask. At that point another mountaineer slithered over the snow bank which almost blocked the door, and with a nod and gruff 'harrumph!' sat down at the farther end of the hut. He was quite short, a little arthritic in his movements, and his face was deeply lined with deep-set, intense eyes that dwelt on you in unnerving, long consideration. His clothes and equipment were, if not actually shabby, certainly well worn and well behind the outdoor fashion of the time. He groped in a pocket for pipe and tobacco and my dog, who was without shame when even the suspicion of food arose, went over to him.

He cursed her for a glutton, whilst at the same time chucking her gently under the chin and playfully shaking her jowls. I offered him coffee, which he accepted, grumbling at the impossibility these days of obtaining anything like quality in that commodity in Britain. He complained aloud that here, of

JOHN LEWIS

Badger-maned, his eyes a glittering blue-grey, John Lewis – sheep-farmer of Tynyfach, Bro Dysynni – pierces me with a fierce look as he growls against European Union regulations and the *Tir Cymen* scheme: 'How long are these people before they're learning the truth. They set stocking rates with no consideration for the farmer, when they should be leaving him to farm the mountain. For the mountain will feed the stock now, but it won't be doing when there is heather and whimberry only, as they're wanting.'

He tells how the number of sheep he runs on the slopes of Cadair Idris has fallen from 1800 to 1470. He's not complaining about lost income – these, he tells me, are comfortable times for the sheep farmer. His concern is for how the mountain will change, how the heather will creep back impenetrably to cover the wide upland pastures. You sense in him the frustration of a man whose family has laboured for generations to create viable pasture from the rough hill, and who is now forced by faceless, ignorant wielders of rules to relinquish a struggle bred into his blood and bone. He moves on into an account of farming up at

Hafodty Gwastadfryn, over 300 metres higher on the flank of the mountain, and suddenly, behind the appurtenances of modern farming, you glimpse a pattern of life which has stretched down the centuries.

The name translates as 'summer house on the flat hill'. All over the Welsh mountains, these ruined *hafodtai* bear witness to transhumance. From the caravan where the house once stood, John and Jac – *y gwas*, the lad, the live-in labourer, a heavy, powerful fifty-year-old who travels back for pub and chapel in his home village of Llan-uwchllyn each weekend, and who has scarcely a word of English on his tongue – carry on the former tradition: 'I take the cattle up there on the 25th of March, and by the 10th of April the mountain is feeding them, and we're giving them no food after that. I saw Jac coming out with two bales of hay when they were grazing the bottoms by the stream and said to him, "Put those back, and if they're still feeding there when we leave, they won't be needing them," and that was on the 3rd of April this year.'

As we sit in his unadorned, modern house, behind the old one and alongside the ruins of the cottage among the beech trees from which, in 1800, Mari Jones began her trek across the hills to Bala to buy her Bible, John takes from a bag a curious set of treasures – *Llyfrau Clustnodau*, ear-mark books. Some are handwritten, others leather-bound mid-Victorian volumes. In them is recorded every stock mark and variation used by every farmer in Wales. Does John know them all? Not, he replies, to describe, but when he sees them by eye, generally then he can tell. The police come to him with stray sheep; he identifies them from the marks, informs the owner and they're collected. Or if they're left unclaimed, they're sold at Dolgellau mart and the proceeds go to local hospitals at Christmas.

He talks of not wanting to exclude, but wishing that those who visited recognized that this landscape is worked, is his livelihood. The irresponsibility that leads to open gates and broken fences involves him in time and expense. And even bodies you might think would behave better are guilty; he positively spits about the activities here of the army. But before the blood-pressure builds, he moves on to tell of his son Richard, farming now at Gwastadfryn: 'The best tractor driver in Wales, and I don't care who knows it. He will go in fields where I wouldn't think of going, knows that tractor to the last ounce of balance. Better on the mechanical than the livestock, but that's the way things are going...'

He lapses into reflective silence. His daughter? She was in the factory in Tywyn, but they made her redundant. She was on the dole for a while, but is now a waitress in a Tywyn cafe. John's wife Winnie comes in with strong tea and thick, buttery slices of delicious *bara brith*. Does he, at sixty-five, have thoughts of retirement? I ask. 'Not a day before I have to,' he responds, combative to the last.

all places, he might have expected to enjoy a solitary pipe on a day like this. I laughed aloud, called him a miserable old sod, told him that for my part too, 'The more I see of humanity, the more I love my dog.' The lines round his eyes deepened still further in amusement, and we set to trading civilized insults directed less personally than against the human race. I knew who he was, recognized him from the author's photograph on the covers of his books, many of which I'd read, and about which I'd formed the opinion that in their restrained, ironic way they were the best body of work yet written about mountain and sea exploration. He was the explorer and mountaineer H. W. Tilman and lived in an elegant Victorian house above the salt marshes on the north bank of the Mawddach estuary outside Barmouth. He pointed the house out to me when we came out of the hut, and invited me to call on him there, which I began to do. Ten o'clock was the time set for arrival, and I soon found out that to be even a matter of minutes late was construed as impolite. At eleven he would make coffee, which came black and bitter in small cups. At twelve he would serve home-made beer, one sip of which confirmed its strength. Lunch was at one, and simple; at two I would go, leaving him, I suspect, to sleep. That was the framework for our meetings.

The content of our conversation was entirely remarkable, and one of the most singular gifts to me. I was in my twenties, embroiled in extreme rock-climbing and the sex, drugs and rock-and-roll lifestyle of those days. He was in his late seventies, one of the legendary figures of mountaineering, with a reputation for austerity, misogyny and profound misanthropy. I found him welcoming, courteous, loquacious, civilized, witty – and also lonely, misunderstood, desirous of explaining the directions of his life. I was, in retrospect, quite insolent in my questioning. Why did you never get married? How can you bear the company of sailors, given Dr Johnson's verdict on them? Is your finest achievement that you have lived to your seventy-eighth year never having had a proper job? How many of these stories about your dislike for your fellow human beings are apocryphal? Tilman didn't mind. He came back at me, invariably sending up the received image of himself, as he did so memorably in the description of himself and Noel Odell on the summit of Nanda Devi, the highest peak in the world to be climbed in the 1930s: 'I believe we so far forgot ourselves as to shake hands on it!' Many of the stories about him come from his long-time expeditionary companion Eric Shipton, who used him as the butt of his humour, but Tilman was perfectly capable of turning that humour on himself:

'By far the greater number of stories told about me *are* apocryphal,' he confided, 'but there is one which is substantially true. It was on an expedition in the 1930s. We embarked at Tilbury, and I stayed on deck until we rounded the North Foreland, whereupon I was heard to mutter the words, "H'm, sea!" I then went below decks and was not seen again until we hove in sight of Bombay six weeks later. I came on deck once more, and was duly heard to utter the words, "H'm, land!" It is asserted that these were the only words I spoke on the entire voyage, which is more or less the truth of the matter, and the reason, quite simply, is that I could not stand the other chaps on that trip.'

He watched to study the effect on me, and dissolved into laughter – but laughter at my puzzled expression, not at his own joke. And the story is a joke, albeit strange and sardonic. From everything I know and have heard and read about Tilman, I'm quite sure it is not literally true. I think now that this man – who as a teenager survived the horrors of the Western Front, fought again with distinction in the Second World War and went on to pursue the most extraordinary career in exploration this century – was presenting me with a parable of his relationship with the world. I never had opportunity to question him again. A few days later, in his eightieth year, he put his dogs in kennels and sailed as an ordinary crew member on a small

OVERLEAF The native Welsh stronghold of Castell y Bere, on the rocky knoll rising from the meadows of Dyffryn Dysynni, guards the approaches to Cadair Idris, on the slopes of which Dafydd, last leader of Gwynedd was betrayed, and over which Mari Jones trudged in 1800 to buy her Bible.

boat bound for the Antarctic. It left Rio on 1 November 1977 for Port Stanley, heading into a season of storms. The rest is silence.

I remember other times on Cadair: running up on a wet autumn day to find as we reached the top the world peeled clean of cloud and gleaming as though renewed; or picking our way down the Fox's Path thirty years ago after the first ascent of one of the hard ice gullies on Cyfrwy, with the sun slanting up the estuary, strewing the slope with fiery rosettes where ice ringed rocks that had melted through the snow. These most beautiful places imprint on our consciousness and in our memory. On this last visit the wind froze fingers and cheekbones, and I shuffled rapidly down to Cyfrwy, whose arête is my favourite way up any mountain (be wary, though – it is most definitely a rock-climb, and of a collapsing variety). It must have been from here that Kilvert's guide pointed out the place 'at the foot of an opposite precipice' where the body of the unfortunate Mr Smith had been found. He was a clerk from Newport on a walking tour of Wales in September 1865, who had disappeared whilst attempting to traverse the mountain without a guide in poor weather and darkness. He was found the following May: 'The foxes and ravens had eaten him. His eyes were gone. His teeth were dashed out by the fall and lay scattered about on the mountain.' I was glad to pass on and race down the broad ridge over Rhiw Gwredydd to follow the route the ponies once climbed, down to the Dysynni valley in the south, and the enclosure and memorial which has been made of the family home of Mari Jones, at the head of Dyffryn Dysynni.

It is a curious kind of memorial to a small event, a small human interchange, which had in its day considerable resonance. The roadside cottage of which it is built must have fallen into decay, but the walls were made good to shoulder height, the chimney-breast and hearth – the *aelwyd* which has meaning among any nation of exiles – rendered sound, and the floor paved evenly with slate, on which has been erected, above a plinth of native stone, a squat pillar of polished brown granite with an open-book motif carved on it. A plaque records the following detail in English and Welsh: 'In memory of

Mari Jones, who in the year 1800 at the age of 18 walked from here to Bala to procure from the Reverend Thomas Charles B.A. a copy of the Welsh Bible. This incident was the occasion of the formation of the British and Foreign Bible Society.'

The incident also became part of the folklore. The Reverend Charles took pity on the girl after her twenty-five-mile walk across the mountains and gave her his own copy of the first cheap edition of the Welsh Bible, the rest having been sold. This was still part of the propaganda in the Sunday schools of my own Manchester childhood. I remember a print of the bare-foot girl poised against the mountain wind, black curls cascading from beneath the hood of her cloak and looking to my ten-year-old eyes just as Kathleen Williams did, whom I sat next to in school and with whom I held hands sometimes in the playground. The extent to which the story has been pared down is striking. Its narrative detail is all moralistic – the girl's arduous devotion, the minister's charity. There is little here to grasp which can give you an understanding of her life. That part of the story has been left hollow and empty as the hearth is now at which presumably she read her Book. You learn more about her from her grave in Bryncrug churchyard, a few miles down the valley, than you do from the shell of Tŷ'n y Ddôl; that she married Thomas Lewis, a weaver, died in Bryncrug on 28 December 1864 aged eighty-two, and was buried at the back of its light, severe chapel above the flood plain of the river by which she grew up, her grave paid for by the Calvinistic Methodists. Bar memory in the region's pubs adds more: an unreliable sense of a woman whom celebrity had turned unpleasant and vain. I prefer to think of her, if indeed she was the agent by which the British and Foreign Bible Society came to be formed, as the instrument also for George Borrow's creation as a writer, for it was his experiences on behalf of the society in Russia and Spain that set him on that track and gave us his masterpiece, *The Bible in Spain*, and two more books, *Lavengro* and *Wild Wales,* which any modern wanderer would be impoverished by not knowing.

Let us leave behind Tŷ'n y Ddôl, with its beech-shaded stream and the

MARTIN RILEY

Canon Martin Riley, Vicar of Tywyn, leans back in a pew in his eleventh-century parish church, and expatiates upon Celtic Christianity – its reverence for nature, the communal life of the *clâs*, or monastic college, its distance from Pauline misogyny and the equilibrium it held between the masculine and the feminine. He's led on by this last into expressing his pleasure in the vote which has just been passed by the Governing Body of the Church in Wales in favour of admitting women into the priesthood, a pleasure he qualifies by reminding of the dangers of triumphalism, and remembering that the hurt felt by those favouring the ordination of women last time would now be felt by those who had opposed it and lost this time.

As this bluff-featured, acute and kindly priest recounts his childhood, the genesis of a capacity to see and feel both sides of an argument becomes apparent. He was born in Caernarfon in 1937, his father the manager of that group of quarries which looks down on to the town from Moel Tryfan and Moel Smytho. The family had left Caernarfon for the quarry village of Penygroes when he was very young, where they lived in a terraced house while waiting for the quarry manager's residence to become vacant. Somehow this never happened, and they'd stayed where they were, in a little house from the back windows of which at clear sunsets you could look out across the Celtic Sea to the Wicklow hills spiky on the horizon.

It's quite clear that he regards this upbringing in a working-class community as a thing of exceptional value. He talks about the influence of the *caban* – the quarry workmen's shelters which at the height of the slate industry's operations became synonymous with the idea of self-improvement – on the cultural life of the village; of the literary and musical attainments of the people of Penygroes and its neighbouring settlements of Talysarn and Nantlle; on the continuing academic success of his old school, Ysgol Dyffryn Nantlle. Were there any difficulties, I wonder, for a manager's son in the playground environment of a working town?

A wry and Christian smile flits across his face, which is answer enough, and he passes on to explain the nature of the call to the ministry – an inner urge, which had always been there, something he knew from the outset. And so, after school, he went to the University College of North Wales, spent too much time playing sport, particularly cricket, which he still enjoys. The David Sheppard of Meirionnydd? Not quite, he admits, and tells of going into services in the church here with his whites on under the surplice after a late finish to a match, and of taking a service once with a broken finger.

The sport, although he enjoys it for its own sake, you sense also to be a means of making contact with young people, building bridgeheads for the Church. And the ethos of the team-game, too, seems for Martin to relate to that of community. He says that modern society's stress on the satisfaction of individual need is difficult to reconcile with responsibility to the community, voices his unease with Mrs Thatcher's excursions into theology and his profound admiration for the social religion of the Rt Rev. David Jenkins. Before he came to Tywyn, his first incumbency was the tiny parish of Beddgelert, where his role was also that of Diocesan Youth Organizer. Now, in what he terms 'Meirionnydd's own Costa Geriatrica', he still works to bring young people under the ethical influence of the Church he loves. And as he speaks, as the keywords – 'reawakening', 'respect', 'ecumenicism', 'the primacy of love' – ring out in his recurrent vocabulary, you feel that, swimming against the social tide though he may be, this genial and understated evangelist might just be having an effect.

old track over the mountain that had taken Mari Jones to unenviable symbolic celebrity, and set off down the valley of the Dysynni. Quiet, broad and green, it's a place of great beauty, and the blue sea glimmers across its end. Craig yr Aderyn rises from sea-level meadows, and cormorants nest here on the rock as they did when the sea lapped its foot. But the valley's most intriguing site is Castell y Bere, the Kite's Castle, built by Llywelyn Fawr in 1221. It was to here that Dafydd retreated after the death of his brother Llywelyn ap Gruffydd in December 1282. The castle was besieged by 3000 men. When the imminence of its fall became obvious, Dafydd escaped – apparently to Dolbadarn – and Castell y Bere fell to the English on 25 April 1283. Dafydd himself was taken prisoner on the slopes of Cadair Idris on 28 June and, as we saw in Chapter Three, was put to death – in the unspeakable manner the English inflicted on those they deemed traitors – on 3 October at Shrewsbury Cross, where a plaque still marks the spot.

Nowadays, no trace remaining of the atrocities of that time, the broken walls of Castell y Bere trail haphazardly around the summit of this surprising rocky outcrop, where the ubiquitous spleenwort grows. A cool wind drifted from the mountain as I entered its green curtilage. Thyme was spreading and violets discreetly blooming. In months to come the delicate harebells would wave here. The place is still. Seven hundred springs have passed since the murderous commotions of war, since the siege and the fall, the blood and the cries at noon. Cloudshadow has passed over, rain, snow and hail fallen. There have been mornings when the valley has been white with frost or filled with mist. Seven hundred times the woods have put forth green leaves. Seven hundred times they have grown tired, faded, burst suddenly into autumn glory and declined into the sodden miseries of winter. There has been human labour and mortality, birth pangs in the cottage by the church below, in the garden of which today a brown-haired woman sits playing a guitar. The first mewling cries of infants have been heard tenderly or with resignation, as have the last breaths of old men whose bodies putrefied and returned to earth to enrich the graveyard loam. The jittering wrens have nested in cracked walls throughout these years, cuckoos called and the cormorants returned to roost on their inland rock as the sea retreated west. The dial on which this valley's time is told has subsumed, rendered insignificant, my time, Mari Jones's time, the time of those who fought, worked, died, were betrayed here, and its hands still sweep on, so that time itself becomes insignificant, and there is only the moment in which, stilled, you see the great calm beauty of process, renewal, decay, in which you see the impersonal force and urge of nature in which I, you, all of us have our part.

A little way past Castell y Bere is a textbook example of river capture. The Afon Dysynni, which has flowed out of Tal y Llyn and which seemed set to continue on its course down the wide, straight fault valley to Tywyn, issues out of a side valley to the south and joins the Afon Cadair. If you follow the Dysynni a mile upstream, it brings you to Abergynolwyn, which has a narrow-gauge railway (like most of the other 'great little trains of Wales', it is a former slate line) and a Railway Inn, which is very local and pleasant. Two miles down the valley, on its south side, the Nant Dolgoch tumbles down a gorge in a pretty series of falls. A path alongside gives out to the track winding through the long upper valley to gain the crest of the stately, untrodden Tarren ridge at Tarren Rhosfarch, whence, if you turn west and keep to the crest, you arrive at the cairn that marks the summit of Tarren Cwm Ffernol. There are two plaques here, which is unusual in the Welsh mountains: the first is a war memorial with a dedicatory line from Winthrop Young to three members of the Mountain Rangers Club who died in the 1939-45 war; the second is to G. H. P. Beames (1906-86), 'founder of the Mountain Rangers Association'. The only other knowledge I possess about this organisation is a piece of paper from a second-hand book, dated July 1936, on which are set out the rules of the Mountain Rangers Club ('founded April 1926'). I have no idea why this place was chosen to commemorate it.

The cairn on Allt Gwyddgwion marks the seaward end of the Tarrens ridge, with little Llyn Barfog, the bearded lake, glinting like a sheet of hammered pewter on the ridge beyond Cwm Maethlon, which for a century and more has been called by the visitors 'Happy Valley'. Below the far ridge are the sand flats of the Dyfi estuary, curving round the brown raised bog of Cors Fochno to the seaside terraces of Borth, which look out, flaking and faded, on to the long, creamy lines of rollers that sweep in under clouds so dark a grey they are almost blue from the wide expanse of Cardigan Bay. The cairn is round and compact and taller than a tall man. It has a speckled appearance from the pieces of quartz used in its construction, which suggests that in origin it is very old, and perhaps a place of a burial – quartz in Celtic countries usually has an association with death and the after-life.

This is the last spur of mountainous upland which Gwynedd throws down to the south-west into the prevailing winds. From here, you descend to Tywyn and a very different landscape – one of those outdated, intriguing little resorts, all Victorian red-brick and wrought iron along safe and extensive sands. It's not somewhere you'd expect to find academic puzzle and historic treasure, but the place has both in the form of a pale crystalline pillar of rock, twenty-five centimetres wide and ten centimetres deep, just over two metres long, and broken into two pieces. It is generally referred to as either the Cadfan or the Tywyn Inscribed Stone. You'll find it in the church (the earlier part of which is lovely in its simple elegance and dates from the twelfth century), where it's been since 1761 – before that it had been used as a gatepost. In the Royal Commission Inventory for Meirionnydd, it's described as 'probably the most ancient monument in the Welsh language'. Scholars date it from the mid-eighth century, making its inscription the earliest written Welsh, of which Ifor Williams, with an ingenuity worthy of the decipherers of Linear B, suggests the following translation: 'Ceinrwy wife

Chapeled and terraced, roofs glistening and chimney smoke rising to mingle with dawn mists, the village of Abergynolwyn – once a quarrying settlement – wakes to its new seasonal tourism role as narrow-gauge railway terminus, trippers now travelling along the line which once carried slates to harbour.

of Addian [lies here] close to Bud [and] Meirchiaw/Cun, wife of Celyn: grief and loss remain/a memorial of four.'

Another early gravestone, its cross very prominent, can be seen in the stonework of the tower beneath the main window on the south side. The church itself was built on the site of a sixth-century *clâs* (monastic college) founded by St Cadfan, who tradition asserts arrived here with a brotherhood of monks from Armorica, and settled by a spring of pure water. In the last century this spring was capitalized on and used as a spa; now it trickles out anonymously somewhere from beneath the concrete floor of the Cadfan Wells Garage. Cadfan ended his life as first Abbot of Ynys Enlli, which is clearly seen on days of good visibility from the beaches of the town. The life of his *clâs* in Tywyn was shared for a while by Deiniol (see Chapter Two), who made his way from here to Bangor. Deiniol's valley itinerary took him via Mallwyd and Llanymawddwy to Bwlch y Groes above Llanuwchllyn, and it behoves us to follow rapidly his route across these southern hills of Snowdonia. The reason for this is readily apparent wherever you glance; it's time, in traversing the southern marches of the National Park, to look more closely at it – afforestation.

Shortly after the Second World War, a government spokesman made the following comment: 'We intend to plant 800,000 acres in Wales. We intend to change the face of Wales. We know there will be opposition but we intend to force this thing through.' The effect of this on the Welsh landscape has been the biggest environmental catastrophe in Britain this century, and one which is only now, as the conifers approach maturity, becoming apparent. Unthinkably large tracts of land in the upland areas of the most beautiful region in Britain have been laid waste. From viable, if marginal, agricultural land which, when properly managed, was a national resource a desert has been created, its onset assured by tax concessions to the most wealthy in our society, its reality concealed for the moment beneath dense coverage of trees. Once the trees have been clear-felled, the true extent of the damage is revealed. Those who, in fifty years' time, view what our generations have allowed to be done will be appalled. As there were those who, fifty years ago, were appalled at the outset. Here's the countryside writer H. J. Massingham, writing about a Welsh valley in 1951:

> ...the hillside was strewn with the fallen logs of former oakwood, this derelict terrain planted up with seedling spruces with the logs left to lie all about them. To any lover of natural beauty the valley would have appeared as transformed from a place of freedom to a prison. It was smothered; it could no longer breathe. The spectacle of this murdered valley is no isolated example.

From Bwlch y Groes and the hills to its east, the murdered valleys lead off by the score: Eunant, Nant y Nadroedd, Nant y Galen, Nant Cwm Lloi – their former life in all its guises has been traduced by the plantations. *'Mangre dawel fynyddig ydyw, lle ardderchog i enaid ddal cymundeb a Duw'* (This is a silent, mountainous retreat, an excellent place for communion with God), O. M. Edwards wrote. This greatest of Welsh educators, whose home was just down Cwm Cynllwyd in Llanuwchllyn, might feel that his motto, *'Codi'r hen Wlad ar ei hôl'* (Raise the Old Country to its former glory), had an ironic ring if he could view now the blighted landscape of his home region.

But for us, the last stage of our journey lies ahead. It takes us down to Llyn Efyrnwy, Liverpool's huge reservoir, built at the end of the last century with the usual disregard for the indigenous community, and inadequate to the city's needs by the middle of this so the process had to be gone through again with similar cost in the flooding of the valley of the Afon Tryweryn. *'Cofia Dryweryn'* reads the fading graffiti you glimpse here and there on bridges and walls – 'Remember Tryweryn'. I wonder what those whose communities were destroyed for the greater good, whose sacrifice or eviction so benefited public utility, would think of the private profit made from water in the last few years? The land surrounding the head of Llyn Efyrnwy is some of the roughest, wildest and – before the construction of forestry tracks in recent years for new plantation – most inaccessible in Wales. The whalebacked heather ridges of Cefn Gwyntog and Cyrniau Nod are nobody's idea of pleasurable leisure; they make the most excruciatingly diffi-cult and arduous walking country. To escape from them down into Pennant Melangell is heavenly release.

This idyllic valley, with its wooden-belfried church, has a legend to suit. It was to here that Melangell retreated, to escape from a marriage her father, an Irish king, sought to impose on her (in one version of the story this was to Iorwerth Drwyndwn, father of Llewelyn the Great). While she is praying one day in her woodland sanctuary, a huntsman, Brochwel Ysgythog, bursts into the clearing with dogs and men in pursuit of a hare, which takes cover under Melangell's gown and stares boldly out at its pursuers. The dogs are urged on, but they cower back. When the huntsman raises his horn to his lips, it sticks to them. Brochwel accedes graciously to the situation and grants Melangell the land and rights of sanctuary. The story is depicted in six wooden carvings in the church, by the east end of which is a shrine above the saint's grave. Inside the church is an effigy with two amusing and vaguely hare-like creatures at its waist. It was a long-standing tradition in the parish that hares were never killed, but since the moors all round the head of the valley have been used as shooting land by psychopathic aristocrats and sadistic business syndicates for almost 200 years, this admirable practice has fallen into abeyance.

Llangynog, two miles down the valley of the Tanat from Pennant Melan-gell, was once an important lead-mining centre, and the footpaths climbing on to the lower slopes of the Berwyn range to the north were connected with the mines. They lead across into the valley of the Afon Rhaeadr, with its seventh-wonder-of-Wales cataract from which the river gets its name (*rhaeadr* means waterfall). George Borrow's much-quoted description of

Pistyll Rhaiadr, highest of Welsh waterfalls, is strangely atmospheric and unexpected at the head of its rising glen in the first high hills a visitor from the east encounters on entering Wales. To George Borrow, who came here in 1854, it resembled the 'long tail of a grey courser at furious speed'.

Pistyll Rhaiadr, Wales's highest waterfall, as the 'long tail of a grey courser at furious speed' is loosely impressionistic rather than precise. The fall is complex. A stream of no great volume spills in three columns which pulse and mingle down a blocky, dark cliff of perhaps 35 metres, efflorescing on the strata and rosetting white against the black rock before a right-hand mossy ridge obscures the water from view and it tumbles into an unseen pool. From here, it sluices sideways through a remarkable round hole in the foot of the ridge to a series of lesser cascades beneath, the general impression being that the fall is less than the 75 metres of its total height. It is the hole and the strange spirit-bridge spanning it that Borrow deplored, which gives Pistyll Rhaiadr its uniqueness and oddly disquieting atmosphere.

The valley above the fall is a quiet, atmospheric moorland place with a stone circle and alignment by the little Afon Disgynfa. As I panted up to the high summits of the Berwyn, I saw black grouse here, and a peregrine chase a skylark, as well as the immediate texture of crystalled, frondy tussocks, red-bladed moor-grass and quartz pebbles in the peat. To the south and east, patchwork valleys lead off to the pastoral shires of England. West and north, fretted across the sunset, are the mountains and valleys of Snowdonia, of which these ridges have given invaders, visitors and homecomers first sight over millennia. Here is the border, there are the hills. Come to know them, their culture and their people with humility, lovingkindness, understanding and respect and your life will be enhanced by them. For all our heedless ravaging, there is still nowhere more beautiful in these islands.

AFTERWORD:
AT CEFN GARW

To end in country where we began, in the Migneint, in fine October weather I walk up the valley of the Afon Serw to Cefn Garw, as I have done many times over many years because to me this place, whose name denotes harsh ridge, is a type of shrine. There are four miles of path or track between it and the narrow moorland road. I know nothing of its history, and there is a part of me is glad it should be so. History, by explaining, complicates, and this is simple, the remotest place.

Always in the approach to it some part of me is hushed, made still: 'Who can deny that things to come are not yet? Yet already there is in the mind an expectation of things to come.' The low house hunches into its ridge, seen from down-valley mistily, its green-hill, faraway presence inexplicable, your eye focused, the closer you approach, to grasp at detail – a sheep-pen wall against the sunset, riddled with light.

Human life has moved on and the natural reclaims. Moss grows across the roof, spleenwort feathers the ridge-tiles, pellets and droppings splash down and mound beneath a gable, cracks jag open at the frost's and wind's behest. As the house fades, the moor grows sleek, a wind preening its blond grasses, tossing its brown heather, the sun tinting it, drawing a blush with its caress from the swell of a slope, a glint in the quartz rock, a glisten on the stream's lips.

That hummocky landscape to the south, broken and uneasy, is where civilization or what we take for it plays peeping Tom on beauty's nakedness - on the hill-brim pylons' and conifers' erectile strut. Can we let well alone or show respect?

Cefn Garw, Migneint, is perhaps the loneliest house in Wales –
one which could stand as the type of Welsh farm left to ruin as the
tide of humanity has drained from these hills, and as symbol of a way
of life, '*Bywyd gwâr mewn bŷd gerwin*' ('a civilized life in a harsh
world'), which also has largely passed.

A knot of baling twine secures the door. A niche in the wall held I know not what, nor do I care. There's stone there now. I come here not for knowledge but for peace. And so I untie the knot. Dry hinges creak to let me enter.

Remnants still used – worm-eaten settle, long tables, blue-painted cupboards of ply with crockery for the shearing, for the day or two each year when life returns: the women here at six, men gathering, whoops and baas, breakfast at eight.

Every year still, dogs scurry and bark, men shout, women laugh and rule in here. Thump of generator, buzz of shears, water boils, knife scrapes on plate, a joust of talk, July dusk, the Land Rovers swaying down the track, a bat's flight fracturing across stillness.

Inside, yellow mural of a ram looks down, painted homage to this way of life. Words too, on every inch of wall: *'Jac Fedw, Dewi Garmon, yn hela llwynog 10/2/80'*, *'Teulu Cefnprys, Llanuwchllyn'* – all nine of them!

But the crog-loft's gone, sky lattices the slates, boards rot, plaster flakes on a lone bedstead, a gap's appeared between two walls, 'Pink Floyd' across the chimney breast, the beam within the inglenook's burnt through, it won't be long...

I spread my sleeping bag across sound boards and step outside. The sun fast-rolling, ridges fade in violet shadow-strata. Within, the moon-faced owl emerges from her roost and with a shake, hush-winged floats down to pass on sighing air. I light a candle here.

Hydref, 1996

SUGGESTIONS FOR FURTHER READING

G. Borrow, *Wild Wales* (Gomer Press, 1995)★†

W. M. Condry, *The Snowdonia National Park* (Collins, 1966)†

W. M.Condry, *Welsh Country Essays* (Gomer Press, 1996)★

A. Conran (trans.), *The Penguin Book of Welsh Verse* (Penguin, 1967)★

P. Crew and C. Musson, *Snowdonia from the Air* (SNP/RCAM, 1996)★

J. Davies, *A History of Wales* (Penguin, 1994)★

A. Griffiths, *Snowdonia: Myth & Image* (Y Lolfa, 1993)★

LL. Gruffydd and R. Gwyndaf, *Llyfr Rhedyn ei Daid* (Gwasg Dwyfor, 1987)

W. J. Gruffydd (ed.), *Math vab Mathonwy* (University of Wales Press, 1928)

E. R. Henken, *Traditions of the Welsh Saints* (Boydell & Brewer, 1987)

H. Hughes and H. L. North, *The Old Churches of Snowdonia* (Jarvis & Foster, 1924)

D. E. Jenkins, *Beddgelert: Its Facts, Fairies & Folklore* (Ll. Jenkins, 1899)

D. Jones, *The Botanists & Guides of Snowdonia* (Gwasg Carreg Gwalch, 1996)★

Gwyn Jones and Thomas Jones (trans.), *The Mabinogion* (Dent, 1949)★†

R. M. Jones, *The North Wales Quarrymen, 1874–1922* (University of Wales Press, 1981)★†

T. Gwynn Jones, *Welsh Folklore and Folk-Custom* (D. S. Brewer, 1979)

F. Lynch, *Gwynedd* (Cadw/HMSO, 1995)★†

P. Monkhouse, *On Foot in North Wales* (Alexander Maclehose, 1932)

J. Morris, *The Matter of Wales* (Oxford, 1984)★

T. Parry (ed.), *The Oxford Book of Welsh Verse* (1962)★†

M. Prestwich, *Edward I* (Methuen, 1988)★

I. B. Rees (ed.), *The Mountains of Wales* (University of Wales Press, 1992)★†

J. Rhys, *Celtic Folklore* (Oxford, 1901)

D. Stephenson, *The Last Prince of Wales* (Barracuda Books, 1983)

S. I. White (ed.), *Bangor: from a Cell to a City* (Friends of Bangor Museum, 1994)★

G. A. Williams, *When Was Wales?* (Penguin, 1985)★

I. Williams, *Enwau Lleoedd* (Gwasg y Brython, 1945)

★ Editions of these titles are currently (1997) in print

† Indispensable reading

GLOSSARY OF WELSH WORDS

aber	river's mouth	*llan*	church, parish
afon	river	*llwybr*	path
bach, fach	small	*llyn*	lake
bwlch	pass, col	*maen*	stone
caer	fort	*mawr, fawr*	big
carnedd	cairn	*moel, foel*	(rounded) hill
castell	castle	*mynydd*	mountain
coed	wood	*nant*	stream
craig	crag	*pen*	top, head
crib	arête, narrow ridge	*pont, bont*	bridge
cwm	valley	*rhaeadr*	waterfall
drws	door, gap, pass	*sarn*	causeway
dyffryn	valley	*traeth*	beach
eglwys	church	*tŷ*	house
hen	old	*ynys*	island

INDEX